THE EDUCATION OF A MUSIC LOVER

THE EDUCATION OF A MUSIC LOVER

A BOOK FOR THOSE WHO STUDY OR TEACH THE ART OF LISTENING

EDWARD DICKINSON

GYAN

Published by

GYAN

Gyan Publishing House
5, Ansari Road
Daryaganj, New Delhi-110002
Phone: 011-47034999, 9811692060
E-mail: books@gyanbooks.com

Distribution Network
gyanbooks.com
India, USA, Canada, UK, Australia

ISBN: 978-93-7225-149-4 (PB)

First Published, 1916

2nd Impression 2026

Printed at: Gyan Press, Delhi.

THE EDUCATION OF A MUSIC LOVER
Author: EDWARD DICKINSON

THE EDUCATION OF A MUSIC LOVER

THE EDUCATION OF A MUSIC LOVER

A BOOK FOR THOSE WHO
STUDY OR TEACH THE ART OF LISTENING

BY

EDWARD DICKINSON

PROFESSOR OF THE HISTORY AND CRITICISM OF MUSIC
OBERLIN COLLEGE

1916

TO

MRS. RUDOLPH BARDENHEUER

PREFACE

> The lost art, that is perhaps nearest of all arts to eternity, the subtle art of listening.
>
> —WILLIAM BUTLER YEATS.

THIS book is an attempt to interpret music to those who already love it upon slight acquaintance and desire the fuller enjoyment that comes with larger knowledge. It is the part of wisdom to make studious preparation for any enterprise that adds to the wealth of the mind, whether it be travelling in foreign lands, looking at pictures, or taking a walk. It is a question of seeing much, of seeing correctly, and of retaining what one sees. With some preliminary acquaintance with the facts of art or nature there is intelligent expectation, and afterward a sense of permanent possession.

It goes without saying that so extensive a survey of musical art as I propose is not intended for those who hear music only for transient, superficial pleasure. Not that I would condemn such pleasure;—the instant joy, the sudden elevation of mood which fine music brings, even to those who know nothing about its principles, is not to be despised; the effect is not altogether evanescent, since every impression upon the senses alters the mental constitution, and even a slight visitation of truth or beauty leaves us a little higher in reason's scale than we were before. But still, this fugitive experience does not quite satisfy a person who is constantly bent on self-improvement, and he will be inclined to ask how he can add something more tangible to his momentary satisfactions, and draw from music that which will call into play his active powers of observation and reflection and give his understanding something solid to feed upon.

The present volume is the result of many years of experience in leading students into the mysteries of music. The writing of it has been especially associated with the very delightful task of interpreting to college men and women the message of the great tone masters from every point of view that may be suggested by their works. In the practice of this lectureship the implied inquiry has always been: What are the elements that music contains in all its phases as an art of design and an art of expression? And also: How much of all this can be understood and appreciated by one who does not sing or play an instrument, and is unacquainted with musical theory? It has been surprising, as well as gratifying, to discover how much of critical appreciation can be developed by an untrained music lover under judicious leadership. This experience has not been isolated, and the success of others in the same undertaking has been such that instruction in what is commonly called "musical appreciation," which has recently become a feature in many conservatories, musical clubs, and private circles, is now slowly making its way into universities, colleges, and public schools. Colleges that are reluctant to establish technical courses in practical music, are beginning to see that the promotion of intelligent taste in music is as much within their province as a similar endeavor in respect to the kindred arts of painting and literature.

In the present volume I have had a mature grade of students, as well as teachers, in mind, for since it is not in any sense a text book, it has seemed best to me to expound music from the higher and more comprehensive point of view, leaving it to those who may do me the honor to read my words to apply its suggestions to their own particular needs and circumstances. Professional musicians will find nothing novel, either in fact or theory; the method of presentation may perhaps contain suggestive features. It is my hope that those who love the art and wish to extend their vision of its beauty, and also those who are trying, systematically or otherwise, to diffuse their love of music over a wider circle, may be helped to obtain a clearer insight into the problems involved, and to catch the enthusiasm which has been the spring and mainstay of the author's labor. My satisfaction will be complete if I have been able to show convincingly that music, rightly pursued, is not only an addition to the gladness of life, but also a means of inward culture.

In the course of the past few years an ingenious

invention has brought the teaching of musical appreciation within the reach of instructors who have sufficient theoretical knowledge. It has made all departments of musical composition in a certain degree accessible even to those who are not expert pianists. I refer to the mechanical piano players, which were at first looked upon with suspicion, and often with abhorrence by professional musicians, but which are proving themselves an agency of immense usefulness in diffusing good music among the people. Those who employ them soon learn that, with skilful handling, these instruments are capable of a large range of expression, and require musical feeling and intelligence for their proper handling. Many musicians have found that it is not beneath their dignity to give instruction in the use of these instruments for the attainment of a correct interpretation of master works. It seems also to be the general testimony that their wide adoption has not diminished the demand for musical instruction by the old established methods. For my own part I am convinced that without this invention lecture courses in the history and criticism of music would have little practical benefit, for it is self-evident that such courses are worthless without abundant illustration. I also feel quite certain that whatever of value this book may contain is multiplied many times by the opportunities for home study which the self-player affords to the amateur.

Some of my readers would probably find my

book practically more convenient if I defined some of the technical terms which I am forced to use. This will be the case, for example, in the division on counterpoint, where fugues are mentioned without explaining what fugues are. But if a beginning were made in defining terms, there would be no end; the book would be perverted into a text book and a dictionary. The few technicalities employed can be elucidated by means of any of the numerous reference books that are always at hand, and accommodating musicians are never far away.

A small part of the substance of this volume has been used in a series of articles in *The Musician* for 1909, and in an address before the Music Teachers' National Association in 1906. This material has been rewritten; by far the greater part is entirely new, and all has been prepared under the guidance afforded by actual experience in the class room.

NORTHAMPTON, MASS.,
August, 1910.

CONTENTS

CHAPTER I

THE NEW MUSICAL EDUCATION

THOSE who love to search for laws and parallels in art history are at times disposed to raise the disquieting question if the flood of musical energy, that has been so steadily rising during the past three or four hundred years, has not reached the high-water mark, or even already begun to recede. Not in quantity, certainly, but in quality, in sheer creative power. The history of art is the history of growth, maturity and decline — not in the productive impulse at large, for art is inseparably identified with human progress, but in its several epochs and departments. Greek sculpture, Gothic architecture, Italian Renaissance painting, Greek and English dramatic poetry, have each in turn exhibited the working of that destiny, beyond the control of men of genius, which decrees that every achievement of the human spirit shall sooner or later exhaust its primal impulse and sink into stagnation, or else into vain repetitions of forms from which all freshness of energy has departed. Are there any signs that the arresting hand of fate has likewise been laid upon the art of tone?

Music has been the latest of the arts to reach maturity. So wonderful have been its achievements that, judging from analogy, it is hardly to be expected that the triumphs of Palestrina and Bach in church music, Beethoven in the symphony, Handel in the oratorio, Schubert in the song, Chopin in piano music, and Mozart and Wagner in the opera can be indefinitely repeated. Up to a recent period we see a progressive evolution of forms and styles. Palestrina and his contemporaries, Bach, Handel, Beethoven, Schubert, Wagner adopted forms that were immature and raised them to fulness of strength. Liszt and Berlioz saw the promise in an old idea, gave it final validity and contrived for it a new form and method. Haydn, Weber, Grieg, and the later Russians went back to the native music of the common people and found there an inspiration that issued in works of novel and exquisite quality. Schumann and Chopin discovered undreamed-of capacities in an instrument already old. Movements parallel to these we cannot discover in our day. The classic forms have been worked out. The promises of the East and North, which a generation ago stirred us with the hope of another musical springtime, have not yet been fulfilled — Tchaikovsky, Dvořák, and Grieg still have no peers among their younger compatriots. A critic of little faith would be inclined to echo the sigh of Mallarmé: "The flesh is sad, alas! and all the books are read."

Certain phenomena, indeed, suggest the approach

of a period of decadence. The spontaneity, the freshness, the directness and inevitableness of utterance which distinguish the work of the men I have mentioned, and indeed of the older masters in general, are certainly not the obvious features in the output of the leading composers of the present generation. Music has become sophisticated and self-conscious. Complication of structure, harmonic strain and stress, superabundance of discord, glaring contrasts, frantic appeals to raw nervous sensation, strive to compensate for a deficiency in vital, original melodic ideas. There is an extreme emphasis upon virtuosity and technical elaboration, which is always an unfavorable symptom in art. Music seems to distrust its own inherent power to satisfy and strives to draw attention by illustrating pictorial or literary subjects, often with a strong attraction toward the extravagant and morbid. Composers in increasing numbers are possessed by the craving for critical self-analysis. They work with calculation. They invent theories which they and their disciples proclaim with tongue and pen. They often seem to go out in deliberate search after originality; they ask not, Is this worth saying? but, Has it been said before? In striving to expand their art, composers of the school of Strauss and Mahler appear to have their minds intent not so much upon the discovery of greater and nobler ideas as upon more gigantic means of expressing their ideas. Individual freedom, the supreme conquest of nineteenth-century art, is after all paying its price. There is no longer a consciousness of mutual support, such as the Renaissance painters found in submission to a prolific common tendency. Even the most sincere and moderate of the later composers are reflective, distinctly aware of the method and purpose of their mental operations. They rarely yield in unquestioning surrender to the guardian genius which drives the artist whither he knows not.

It would be rash to assert that these appearances are necessarily signs of impending decrepitude. They may indicate the need of a period of rest and recuperation, of reaction toward the simpler ideals of an earlier time. Perhaps, on the other hand, they indicate that new materials are being gathered for the use of strong men soon to come. The harmonic experiments of the Debussys and Ravels, like the experiments of the Impressionists with pigments and of the Symbolists with words, may prove the means of enlarging the technique for the service of wider expression. But at any rate the youthful period of music is past, and the art has attained full strength and stature. The only question is, how long will the period of maturity last? Will new nations — our own perhaps, an emancipated Russia, or it may be the awakening peoples of the Orient — applying the fully developed European technique to ageless stores of emotional experience, instil into the veins of music a new energy which centuries only can exhaust?

Those who look for a check in the progress of

music on the creative side may easily console themselves by the thought that there is no sign of abatement in the spread of its beneficent influence. Whether or not the works of the past are to be equalled or excelled, the problem of the adaptation of music to the spiritual and intellectual needs of men still waits for solution. An epoch of fuller knowledge and appreciation on the part of both musicians and the public seems plainly to be at hand. The waning of the productive energy would not be altogether a cause for lament if thereby the world could be turned to a deeper love and understanding of the treasures it already possesses. And the grounds for such hope are multiplying daily. There can be no question that the sum of musical intelligence is vastly greater the world over than it was fifty years ago. In the very midst of the era of artistic fecundity the epoch of scholarship and enlightenment has become established. The nineteenth century has seen the founding of many musical educational institutions, administered in accordance with the highest standards of discipline and research. Every department of musical history, æsthetics, science, and technical application has been investigated by scholars of Germany, France, England, and other countries with an exactness, a precision, and a breadth of vision that are not surpassed in any field of learned inquiry. The methods of teaching in composition and performance have been reconstituted on a basis of thoroughness which leaves nothing to be desired, except that constant revision and refinement of method which in music as in all education is an endless process. Text books and treatises on every conceivable musical subject increase beyond all computation. The great composers are subjected to an exhaustive review, ranging from minutest textual examination to emotional interpretation. This spirit of earnestness is pervading all classes. The provincial music teacher has caught the contagion and the desire for accuracy and system is spreading to the musical frontiers, revolutionizing the whole scheme of musical instruction. "Twenty-five years ago," says a recent English writer, "what were called 'lessons' were given, as they are now; but in the old days, while the lessons were given, nothing was taught. Music was not part of a serious education; it was a fashionable accomplishment. . . . Such a method, if method it may be called which was none, is now changed for a full, rational, and liberal study, carried on just as thoroughly, as intellectually, and as systematically as in any other serious branch of learning." Not less remarkable has been the educational progress in music in this country. The advance that has been made in the last thirty years is little short of revolutionary. The true measure of the nation's advancement toward the proud distinction of being a musical people does not consist in the number of operas given in New York in a season, nor in Paderewski's income from a single concert tour, nor even in the amount of respectable compositions produced by native musicians, but rather in the extent to which good music is becoming a necessity in the life of the community.

Accepting such a standard there is every reason for gratification and hope. Those who love music for what is best in it are rapidly increasing in number. The educative value of music is widely recognized. Performers, directors, and teachers find every day more encouragement for solid work. The musical magazines that devote themselves to strictly educational questions receive generous support. Publishing houses find a large demand for critical works on musical subjects of every description. Men of superior mental attainments are giving themselves in increasing numbers to the service of the higher musical propaganda. Through the wide world of musical dilettantism is felt the bracing influence of a better purpose. It is easy to overlook these signs of promise in view of the vast abundance of musical vulgarity, encouraged and delighted in by multitudes both high and low. The cheap graphophone, the vaudeville, the musical comedy and the "popular" song seem to many observers representative of the musical taste of the future as well as of the present. In the babel of discordant sounds the voices of those who proclaim the gospel of sweetness and light in musical art often sound faltering and far away. But over against this wide-spread satisfaction with the tawdry and vulgar must always be recognized that conspicuous trait in the American character upon which reformers of every sort have learned to rely — an intellectual unrest, a craving for new ideas, a respect for things of the mind, a readiness to be led in the direction of better individual and social accomplishment. The progress of music in America is simply a detail of the rapid advancement in the appreciation of fine art, and its application in the adornment of public and private life, which is one of the most auspicious phenomena of the present day. Let any one read a few pages in the history of American music, compare the programs of Thalberg in the '50's with those of Paderewski in the '90's, observe the results of the missionary labors of such men as Lowell Mason, Theodore Thomas, Carl Zerrahn, and Thomas Ryan, glance over the musical programs of our leading churches and compare them with the practice of forty years ago, count the catalogues of the music schools and peruse their contents, note the increase of orchestras and choral societies, learn what some of our cities are doing for the musical welfare of the people, consider the attention that is given to music in the public schools and colleges, try to form an estimate of the number of musical clubs and the measure of their influence. After such a survey no excuse could be found for discouragement on the part of any one who is engaged in the effort to make music a living force in national life.

As a result of these tendencies of the last few decades, musical education in this country has now entered upon a new stage of its career. Having reformed its methods, elevated its standards, and thrown wider the doors of opportunity, all in the interest of the special student, it is now turning its favor toward those who stand outside the ranks of those who would play, sing, or compose, the noble company upon whom music depends for its patronage, the expectant majority represented by the dilettante, the amateur, the actual or potential music lover. It is shaping its plans and adjusting its methods with a view to the extension of taste and appreciation among the people. Its ultimate purpose is to promote intelligent musical enjoyment as a factor in popular education.

In the history of music up to a recent time the cultivation of taste on the part of the public, and even on the part of individual pupils, has commonly been left to take care of itself, as a sort of by-product rather than a primary intention. Training has been directed toward what is called "practical" musical instruction, viz. playing, singing, and composing. Systematic cultivation of æsthetic taste in schools and colleges by means of the critical study of masterworks has been confined to literature, perhaps because literature is a form of expression with which every educated person comes into personal relations in the natural order of his life. In the English-speaking countries this has especially been the case, for the artists around whom patriotic pride has gathered have been, with a few exceptions, poets and novelists, rather than painters, sculptors, or composers. The conception of art is very largely made to conform to a literary standard; art, it is thought, must convey "ideas," by which is meant lessons, appeals, admonitions that can also be expressed in words; pictorial or musical impressions are esteemed of minor significance, and the inevitable inclination is to translate them into verbal terms, under a sort of blind notion that to do so gives them a practical instead of a questionable value. The result has been that the great majority of those who deal with music only as hearers have been left to gain what knowledge and taste they could by the casual attendance upon concerts and opera performances, and by reading musical criticisms in the newspapers. The latter means of enlightenment is manifestly incomplete, since musical reviews in the daily press are concerned with the merit and demerit of performances or of new compositions—that is, the application of general principles to concrete cases—almost never with the discussion of the general principles themselves. Consequently the history of music shows us by a thousand instances—often very melancholy instances—that the taste of the public has usually acted as a drag upon musical progress. Appreciation of art must always, of course, lag behind artistic creation; it is one aspect of that conservative element in the human compound which, as a check upon overhasty radicalism, is an undoubted advantage to the race. None the less are popular ignorance and prejudice in matters of reason and imagination to be deplored, and a movement to develop an appreciation of what is beautiful and profitable in art must certainly, to employ the threadbare phrase of the newspapers, "meet a long felt want."

This movement is now well under headway and its promoters cannot be accused of a lack of zeal. A well known critic writes a book entitled "How to Listen to Music," parallel to those useful manuals, "How to Study Pictures" and "The Appreciation of Sculpture." Another publishes a volume in answer to the question, "What is Good Music?" Two others explain essentials of form under the title, "The Appreciation of Music." These works are but samples of a whole library aiming directly or indirectly at a similar purpose. The musical magazines are giving larger space to matters of broad musical culture as compared with the discussion of pedagogic subjects, and the literary periodicals are feeling the stress of this new interest. Musicians everywhere are adding instruction in criticism and interpretation to their office as practical trainers. Already specialists in this new field are beginning to appear. Most significant and promising of all, this department of education is planting its feet in universities, colleges, seminaries, and public schools. It has been discovered that a critical discrimination can be imparted in respect to music as well as in literature, and by analogous methods; and with the influence of institutions of learning thrown into the scale the hope for the advancement of a higher musical culture among the educated classes rises to confidence. With music becoming a national concern, administrators of colleges and schools find it a part of their duty to direct it, so far as lies within their power over young minds, toward the ends of individual and collective benefit.

It was unquestionably their doubt in regard to the intellectual and disciplinary value of music that so long hindered school boards and college trustees from uniting musical instruction with their orthodox schemes of classroom and laboratory work. They said implicitly to the music teachers of the country: Gentlemen, show us that your methods are based on thoroughly scientific foundations and that the results furnish a fair parallel to those that are expected from the established school and college courses, and then we will consider the question of opening our doors. This the leaders of musical education have done. The long resistance of college and school has begun to yield. The question now is not whether music is worthy of admission to the academic precincts, but exactly what office shall be assigned to her in coöperation with the classic sisterhood of arts and sciences. The institutions that have taken music into their folds have already divided her service into two departments—she is used as a means of promoting æsthetic culture and appreciation among many, as well as training productive and executive faculties on the part of a few.

All college studies are contained in two classes —vocational studies and culture studies. Music, by its very nature, belongs to both. As this whole book is devoted to music as a culture study, the distinction between the two classes need not be enlarged upon here. Neither does it seem to me to require argument to prove that the dissemination of good taste in art is an obligation upon college and school. If such argument is needed, there is no better summary than that of President Frederick Burk of the San Francisco State Normal School. "The world," he says, "uses vocations as a means of bread winning, but the world also uses music, art, literature, the drama just as intensely, just as essentially, just as relevantly. Because the world uses religion, art, music, the drama, civic ideals, etc., these are as legitimate and important goals of education as bread winning."

This interest in the extension of musical appreciation, once taking root as a conviction, becomes an enthusiasm. It is by no means confined to university circles. Nowhere is it more beautifully manifested than among the noble group of obscure private teachers, who at stated times gather their little company of pupils and talk to them on the deeper things of their art. This is indeed a service that "blesseth him that gives and him that takes."

There is no need to search for the motives that impel so many teachers, lecturers, and magazine writers to preach the pure gospel of musical art, but I love to think that here is shown one phase of the humanitarian movement of the time. In every earnest heart there is an instinctive desire to communicate to others its own experiences of good. And so when music is felt by one of its votaries to be a source of unalloyed happiness and purification of spirit he is fired with something like a missionary zeal. He catches the philanthropic vibration that is abroad in the air. He too would be a social benefactor. He would bring the sweet companionship of music into the common life as a means of effecting a closer fellowship of minds in the higher regions of sentiment.

"We who care deeply about the arts," says the Irish poet, William Butler Yeats, "find ourselves the priesthood of an almost forgotten faith, and we must, I think, if we would win the people again, take upon ourselves the method and the fervor of a priesthood." It is well said, and those who are girding themselves for this high service of proselytism may well bethink themselves of their qualification for the mission. Consecration—yes, a priest must have that, together with a willingness to undergo resistance, indifference, and the trials of hope deferred. But he must likewise possess knowledge and wisdom—knowledge of the truth he teaches so that his own faith will not be shaken, knowledge of the needs and aptitudes of those among whom he labors, and the wisdom which enables him to adapt the means to the end, and to seek that end on the higher levels and not the lower.

Let us go on, then, to consider what are the problems involved and the methods by which a better and more accurate understanding of the joyful mysteries of music can be imparted to those who desire a fuller experience of the pleasures and benefits of musical art.

CHAPTER II

THE MUSIC LOVER'S NEED OF EDUCATION

THE necessity of instruction in the art of hearing music can hardly be denied by one who thinks about the matter. It is not alone the "masses" who are ignorant, and in their ignorance judge foolishly. A large number who call themselves educated must be included among those who are outside the kingdom of music. The scorn of the musical experts for the taste of those they serve has been, and is even now, more or less outspoken, and it would require a wide stretch of charity to say that it has not been justified. The history of musical patronage, so often clogging the wheels of achievement, is a painful one when it is observed how many of the noblest spirits in the realm of art have suffered and even perished because of public dulness or intolerance. There has certainly been a vast improvement; there is immense encouragement to be found by comparing the records of the present with the annals of, say, fifty or seventy-five years ago; then far more than now empty virtuosity flourished without check and with little rebuke. But still, if it were possible to apply tests among the habitués of opera houses and concert halls by which those could be discovered who perceive in music its central qualities as fine art, refusing to be deceived by the sensational, temporary, and meretricious, a sanguine investigator would probably experience sad disillusion. It is the conclusion of one of the foremost American musical authorities, after a quarter of a century of observation, that among the frequenters of musical performances hardly one in a thousand knows what good playing or singing really is. This, of course, is an exaggeration, thrown out in one of those dark hours which sometimes come to the musical illuminati when for a whole season, seated upon the Olympian heights of criticism, they have surveyed the delusions of the populace below. But it is sufficiently near the truth to pass with only a moderate qualification. Now if the elements of good performance, which are really so simple and obvious, are unknown to the average concert goer, how much more certain is it that the criteria of merit in composition will be obscure to him. A high degree of intelligence in other departments of art is no guarantee of musical understanding. Underlying the ignorance of musical principles is the fundamental ignorance that music has any principles that are necessary to be known by one who lays claim to culture. Music suffers like the drama from the common use of it among intelligent people for recreation and amusement, rather than as something intellectually profitable and demanding serious mental application as its right. No one can enjoy a feeling of ease in cultivated society who has not at least a casual acquaintance with the great poets and romancers, and an impression of the work of the chief painters and sculptors of the world. An utter lack of acquaintance with the masters of music, however, is often the ground for complacency or even of pride. A recent work on æsthetics by a well-known university professor contains a blunder on a point of music which would certainly not have been paralleled if a matter connected with literature or any other department of art had been in question. Bruneau tells us that it was quite characteristic of the taste of the period that when Rossini's "Otello" was produced in Paris (the first performance was in 1821), nobody objected to the bacchic joy of the songs, the delirious gayety of the orchestra, the nonsense of the *vocalises* applied during three acts to the terrible drama of hatred and love. Even literary men, like Lamartine, de Musset, and Stendhal, who knew and admired Shakespeare, were fired with enthusiasm at the representations of this parody of the venerable masterpiece. Rossini's "Otello" is long dead and no works of its kind are likely to appear again, but the literati can hardly take credit to themselves for the prevalence of a taste which prefers the "Otello" of Verdi to its predecessor.

When it comes to a comprehension of music as

a fine art a large proportion of the literary class are represented either by Dr. Johnson or by Boswell. When the great lexicographer was seventy-one years of age he chanced one day to hear some funeral music, and remarked that it was the first time that he had ever been affected by musical sounds. Boswell was more susceptible. "I told him," said the faithful scribe on another occasion, "that music affected me to such a degree as often to agitate my nerves painfully, producing in my mind alternate sensations of painful dejection, so that I was ready to shed tears; or of daring resolution, so that I was inclined to rush into the thickest part of the battle." "Sir," said Johnson, "I should never hear it if it made me such a fool." Between Johnson's indifference and Boswell's sentimental excitability the wise man would, perhaps, find little to choose. The true nature of music's virtue probably had never dawned upon either of them. Boswell, indeed, possessed a source of pleasure unknown to his friend, but his nervous explosions would hardly leave any very valuable deposit behind them. If he described his mental condition accurately the effect of music upon him was of the most indefinite and transient character. And so it is upon the minds of a vast number of people who call themselves musical, and give concerts and operas their regular attendance. The impression they receive is hardly more distinct than that of a succession of perfumes; the subsequent memory is that of something exhilarating but vague, like a last week's display of fireworks. Outside of the hall or theatre they give no study to the scientific principles of musical art or its psychologic reactions, and consequently their judgments, if that term can properly be applied, are unconsidered and usually perverse, since they are touched off by the mere nerve stimulation of the instant. Such indulgences in pleasant sound have, indeed, a value to those who come jaded with prosaic toil; like coolness after summer heat they bring repose and refreshment and are vastly to be preferred to many of the fashionable distractions of the hour. But to one who knows the benefits which music can impart—that its tonic properties have it in them to restore the worn spirit and inform and enrich the mind at the same time—there comes often a feeling of pain that the greater good should not be enjoyed at the same time with the lesser.

Among those who receive music in a general way there is a class of minds, very serious and philosophical, to whom the very vagueness of these diffused impressions seems the condition of the most inspiring communications. These thinkers, mystical in temperament and introspective in habit, discern in music a spiritual suggestion more eloquent than speech, whose very indefiniteness and unreality impart to it a sublimated value. In many such cases the effect upon the imagination seems in inverse ratio to the amount of artistic contrivance involved in the music; the mere physical sensation of tone even with slight dynamic fluctuations is sufficient to produce powerful emotional reaction. To Thoreau any sound that could be called musical disturbed his thought with a sense of something ineffable. A music box is tinkling near by, and he writes in his Journal: "I feel a sad cheer when I hear those lofty strains, because there must be something in me as lofty that hears." Again he confesses: "I hear one thrumming a guitar below stairs. It reminds me of moments that I have lived. What a comment upon our life is the least strain of music! It lifts me above the mire and dust of the universe. . . . Ninety-nine one-hundredths of our lives we are mere hedgers and ditchers, but from time to time we meet with reminders of our destiny. We hear the kindred vibrations, music! and we put our dormant feelers into the limits of the universe. We attain to wisdom that passeth understanding." Two days later he makes this entry: "What is there in music that it should so stir our deeps? Suppose I try to describe faithfully the prospect which a strain of music exhibits to me. The field of my life becomes a boundless plain, glorious to tread, with no death nor disappointment at the end of it. All meanness and trivialness disappear."

To this man who had kept his sensibilities so delicate and pure, so responsive to every touch of nature, the mere impact of tone upon the ear was equivalent to an ecstasy. The "telegraph harp" contained the essence of symphonies and oratorios and made them superfluous. Reading these testimonies of Thoreau we can in a measure understand how to the Greek philosophers the simplest unharmonized strains contributed to ethical and emotional culture, and thus had a place in the scheme of education.

To a philosophic poet like Browning, who united the gift of intuitive vision with a rare power of reflective analysis, the sounds of music excite conjecture over the ultimate cause of that rapture which no other art can arouse in equal measure. In "Parleyings" with Charles Avison, Browning speaks what is thus far the last word in occult musical interpretation. Music reveals the Soul — the sum of those mysterious faculties that compose the subconscious personality; Mind works consciously, builds up knowledge with the facts of experience, as an engineer builds a bridge over a gulf, laying stone upon stone. Beneath rolls something that Mind may hide but not tame—"Soul, the unsounded sea," whose "lift of surge" brings feeling from out the depths which Mind cannot master. Mind's processes are easy to describe;

> "But Soul's sea — drawn whence,
> Fed how, forced whither, — by what evidence
> Of ebb and flow, that's felt beneath the tread,
> Soul has its course 'neath Mind's work overhead, —
> Who tells of, tracks to source the founts of Soul?
>
> . . . .
>
> "To match and mate
> Feeling with knowledge, — make as manifest

Soul's work as Mind's work, turbulence as rest,
Hates, loves, joys, woes, hopes, fears that rise and
sink
Ceaselessly. . . .
"To strike all this life dead,
Run mercury into a mould like lead,
And henceforth have the plain result to show —
How we Feel hard and fast as what we Know —
This were the prize and is the puzzle! — which
Music essays to solve."

Music comes nearest to realizing the desire of all art, to make the work of the Soul as manifest as the work of the Mind; she seems about to give momentary feeling permanence, to unveil our hidden impulses and motives; but the very essence of her nature, her fluidity and quick vanishing into the impalpable inane, forbids.

"Could music rescue thus from Soul's profound,
Give Feeling immortality by sound,
Then were she queenliest of arts. Alas —
As well expect the rainbow not to pass."

Lafcadio Hearn, convinced of the Buddhist doctrine of metempsychosis, is drawn by music into the illimitable ocean of Being composed of billions of pre-natal memories. "To every ripple of melody, to every billow of harmony, there answers within, out of the Sea of Death and Birth, some eddying immeasurable of ancient pleasure and pain. Pleasure and pain: they commingle always in great music; and therefore it is that music can move us more profoundly than any other voice can do. . . . It is only the sum of the pains and joys of past lives innumerable that makes for us, through memory organic, the ecstasy of music. All the gladness and the grief of dead generations come back to haunt us in countless forms of harmony and melody."

Such experiences, which are transmuted into poetry by men like Thoreau, Browning, and Hearn, are not to be lightly spoken of. They stir the emotions to depths which no other excitation can reach. They are akin to religious ecstasies, and it is in recognition of certain correspondences in our nature that the church has always welcomed the aid of music in its efforts to draw the devotee into a charmed circle from which earthly associations shrink away. The practical musician, however, has accustomed himself to take the matter more coolly. While not denying that these mystical transports are legitimate and the source of a joy that is at the same time elevating and purifying, still he distrusts them and would never admit that the aim of musical study is to make one more susceptible to them. It is evident that if musical enjoyment began and ended with emotional stimulation of this kind the critical study of music would be merely the study of psychologic reactions, and not at all a study of laws and methods by virtue of which music becomes a fine art based on scientific principles and appealing to the intellect as well as to the sense. There would be no guarantee of any objective standard of merit or demerit; the strumming of a guitar which stirred such high contemplations in Thoreau, if measured by its effects alone, might outbalance in his mind an orchestra playing the Andante from Schubert's "Unfinished" symphony. In the case of weaker minds, those endowed with an excess of sensibility over judgment, music is often the parent of effeminate sentimentalities which, if habitually indulged, produce those relaxing results of which moralists complain. Where the purely subjective interpretation has free sway, minds less robust than those of Thoreau and Browning may receive less noble suggestions. It is in vain to search in sudden excitements, which may move in exactly contrary directions at different times of the day or with changing conditions in the nervous system, for any guidance that may enable the hearer to distinguish good music from bad. Neither do they involve a definite conception of a musical composition as a concrete work of art. The delight of the moment at the train of associated ideas may be recalled in faded colors, but no memory of a thing in itself beautiful in design and execution.

Just here a qualification must be made, lest I be misunderstood and be classed among the pedants. The raptures such as Milton felt, when the floods of glorious tone dissolved him into ecstasies and brought all heaven before his eyes, not only afford us some of the happiest moments of our existence, but when rightly adjusted to our other experiences may become a source of moral refreshment and strength. There is in music preëminently a beauty of spiritual intimation, of mysterious goings to and fro in the dim passages of memories and hopes, of mirth and tears, of associations indefinable but allied to what we feel to be the best there is in us. A poet like Lafcadio Hearn, who catches in music a reverberation of the joys and sorrows of all mankind, receives a truer communication than the bookish technician who perceives nothing but skilful devices in theme development, counterpoint, or orchestration. I would not disparage those delights that come with unformed sound (unformed, I mean, so far as the listener is aware) any more than I would disown the joy in the murmur of winds and waves and the songs of happy birds. We accept them as tokens of health in the universe, and it is a sign of health in ourselves that we exult in them. Doubtless all pure sounds have a significance in our soul life which philosophy has not yet explained. So in music the passionate response of the heart to beauty is the ultimate thing, and in these moments of abandonment learned science and theory may well be left behind. But neither of the two opposed methods of reception—the half-hypnotized absorption and the cold critical analysis—is sufficient alone. Only one who is capable of both is competent to receive all that music has to give. Knowledge and feeling must unite. At the moment of hearing, feeling seems to have it all her own way, but it is the antecedent knowledge that directs feeling so that she may not go astray and waste herself on what is unworthy. Reason must hold the helm. Music, like all fine art, demands an active exercise of the will, as well as a sensitiveness to physical elements and a vague response to suggestion.

The first business of a lover of art is to sharpen his faculties of perception. The eye and the ear must be trained to quick discriminations, and these discriminations must be controlled by preliminary knowledge of the function and method of the art in question, in view of the character and limitation of its material and the range of effect permitted by its subject matter. The beauties to which the untrained mind is most alive are those of physical sensation and associative suggestion; those which it fails to observe lie in form, proportion, design, mutual adaptation of details to the central purpose—that is, beauties of workmanship. The discipline that one must undergo in order to appreciate fine art is largely an exercise of eye and ear, reënforced by the power of coördination, in order that simple sensations may group themselves into images which are the media or the garments of thought.

Never in art can "thought" and "form" be severed; least of all in music. The artist's vision becomes clear to himself only as he laboriously puts it into form, and his intention becomes clear to us also in the extent to which we are able to follow his processes. A work of art possesses an objective as well as a subjective value. It stirs the imagination and opens depths of human emotion not sounded before; but it also offers delight to the physical eye or the physical ear, and likewise gratifies the intellect when there is seen a masterly adaptation of means to ends. The artist is a craftsman as well as a seer. The original conception comes to his mind as a germ, not as a complete organism. He devotes all his ability to the deliberate shaping of his materials, and invents patterns that are in themselves beautiful apart from any associated meaning that may be stated in words. There is a decorative beauty in every art-work as well as a beauty of sentiment. From a purely ornamental design, such as a Rookwood vase or an architectural moulding, to a sonnet of Wordsworth or Rembrandt's etching of the Prodigal Son, where the technical element seems lost in the nobility of the thought, there is every degree of emphasis upon the decorative factor. The artist never forgets this, and without an appreciation on our part of the balance of rhythmic phrase and juxtaposition of euphonious words, or the artful arrangement of lines and groups and masses, the artist's purpose, so far as we are concerned, is not achieved.

This decorative feature — using the term in its largest sense — marks out one of the paths along which the learner's study must be persistently directed. If his senses are not trained to discern the manifold beauties that are contained in design and technical manipulation, his judgments will have no secure basis and the very essential of æsthetic appreciation will elude his grasp. His perception of moral values may be exquisitely refined, his heart may beat sympathetically to many notes of rapture or pain, and still a whole world of loveliness be closed to him. With attention fixed only upon subject and sentiment, he would perhaps be content with ignorant and awkward execution if the theme appealed to his religious, patriotic, or domestic affections. There are, of course, possible deficiencies on the other side, for which no delicacy of perception, no learning in technique, can compensate. The connoisseur who sees nothing in Millet's "Sower" but a superb representation of bodily action is to be pitied for his narrowness of mental vision. When Whistler labelled his portrait of his mother an "arrangement in black and gray," on the ground that no one would be interested in the sitter as an individual, but that a skilful contrast of tones was all that an instructed lover of art ought to care for in such a composition, he carried his pet theory to an extreme where those who feel art most deeply are reluctant to follow. All this may be admitted, and still the fact remains that the decorative value in art is the feature in which the great majority even of intelligent people most need to be instructed. The force and subtlety of Whistler's portrait are unquestionably affected by the simplicity of the scheme of lines and the arrangement of the sombre shades. The drawing and composition of Raphael, the chiaroscuro of Rembrandt, the atmosphere of Corot are the very life of the works of these men; they are ends as well as means; without them there would be no individuality, no personal communication. They are elements which, if they could be completely severed from subject, would still be worthy artistic aims. The mutilated fragment known as the "Torso Belvedere," from which all definite expression of character has departed with the loss of head and limbs, was nevertheless the object of the loving study of Michelangelo.

Say what we may in regard to ideas, emotion, the infusion of personality as the aim and justification of art, still we must not lose sight of the fact that the supreme artists of the world — the Shakespeares, the Michelangelos, the Beethovens — were consummate masters of technique, and only through sovereign technique could they impart their thought and realize their visions. There is no more common error than to suppose that these men and others of the same rank were superior as artists because they felt more and deeper than other men. The difference is not in feeling but in the ability to incorporate feeling in artistic form. It is absurd to suppose that Winslow Homer felt the appalling strength and infinite beauty of the sea more than other painters who failed in the attempt to render them. The "mute inglorious Milton" of Gray never existed. If one is a Milton he will not be mute. Says Ruskin: "Weak painters, who have never learned their business, continually come to me crying out, 'Look at this picture of mine; it *must* be good, I had such a lovely motive. I have put my whole heart into it, and taken years to think over its treatment.' Well, the only answer for these people is, 'Sir, you cannot think over anything in any number of years—you haven't the head to do it; and though you had fine motives, strong enough to make you burn yourself in a slow fire, if only first you could paint a picture, you can't paint one, nor half an inch of one; you haven't the hand to do it.' "

It is indeed the hand, as well as the head and the heart, that makes the artist, and the knowledge of the part played by the hand is indispensable to one who aspires to become a connoisseur. The mysteries of craftsmanship are not intuitively discerned, and the uninitiated never perceive them. Appreciation is not passive, like a simple sensation; and it is the result of effort and judicious training. If a casual lover of pictures were to walk through an art gallery with Mr. Edwin Blashfield or Mr. Lorado Taft he would soon discover that his own world of æsthetic experience was a very limited affair compared with that of his companion. The difference is well illustrated by a passage in Mr. Kenyon Cox's essay on Rodin in his *Painters and Sculptors.* He is speaking of the statue called "The Danaïd," and describes it as "a single female figure about half the size of life, fallen forward in an odd, half-crouching attitude expressive of utter despair or of extreme physical lassitude." The average gallery habitué, interested in whatever belongs to life but ignorant of the "points" of good sculpture, would be attracted by the title, would inquire concerning the story of the Danaïds, and if a person of sensibility would be touched by the suggestion of pathos, and would perhaps notice certain graces of proportion which the figure offered to his sight. But now, as Mr. Cox proceeds, notice what a trained critic sees in this statue: "Everything is largely done, with profound knowledge, the result of thousands of previous observations, and the significance of every quarter-inch of surface is amazing. Such discrimination of hard and soft, of bone and muscle and flesh and skin, such sense of stress and tension where the tissues are tightly drawn over the framework beneath, such sense of weight where they drag away from it—all this is beyond description as it is beyond praise. And it is all done with admirable reticence, without the slightest insistence or exaggeration, and with such a feeling for the nature of the material employed that the marble seems caressed into breathing beauty, its delicate bosses and hollows so faintly accented that the eye alone is hardly adequate to their perception and the finger-tips fairly tingle with the desire of touch."

Here is the report of a connoisseur who has acquired the ability to distinguish beauties that lie in the material and the methods of sculpture, beauties that would never be seen by an observer whose culture was general and not special. Similar lessons may be drawn from the testimony of those who have made music a life study. Their advantage lies primarily in the fact that, by reason of their knowledge of the nature of musical structure and the laws of performance, their minds are set at such a focus that the qualities of the composition make a clear and logical impression. The critic applies the standards that are pertinent to the case; he grasps the details in proper order and sees how they contribute to fulfil the composer's structural design and emotional conception. His hearing has become discriminative through his experience with works and principles; he knows what to look for, and can grasp relationships as well as perceive details. His memory has acquired possession of many masterpieces which he is able to compare with one another, and also to use as touchstones in the appraisal of other claimants upon his favor. Out of this discipline comes judgment, and finally taste with its exhaustless resources of pleasure.

A frequent objection to technical study rests upon the fact that increase of knowledge in matters of art brings with it certain penalties. In ascending from the plane of lower to that of higher pleasures one seems doomed to leave behind certain naïve enjoyments that arise from a frank and childlike acceptance of everything that gives agreeable stimulation to the organs of sight and hearing. As one leaves the condition of paradisaical innocence and approaches critical enlightenment one becomes aware of evil as well as of good; there are shocks of disappointed expectation, followed by sourness and asperity instead of that joy and peace which seem the just recompense of one who goes in quest of beauty. The professional critic is not envied by the art loving public. His calling is supposed to promote an excessive irritability of nerve, an unhealthy tendency to ignore the good and magnify the evil, a habit of fault finding until fault finding becomes a pleasure. No honest critic will admit the justice of such an imputation, yet even he sometimes questions if the pains do not overbalance the rewards. Even so magnanimous a spirit as Mr. E. A. Baughan has sometimes at the end of a season entertained the disquieting suspicion that, after all, ignorance is really bliss and that wisdom may sometimes run to the excess that verges upon folly. But the critic so minded does not know his own blessedness. He has sources of satisfaction of which the Philistine who "knows nothing about art but knows what he likes" has very little conception. The critic enjoys more than the other because he sees and hears more, and is better prepared to grasp the real significance of what he sees and hears. His occasional distress is only the reverse side of his enjoyment. The cheap popular march or sentimental ballad irritates him just because an étude by Chopin or a song by Grieg makes him so happy. There is even a not ignoble pleasure in his very distaste, because there cannot be a revolt against stupidity and vulgarity without comparison, and comparison involves even at the moment an under-consciousness of merit elsewhere. There are critics and critics. The true critic is one who sees below the surface of things, distinguishes the essentials from the accidents, the spirit within the form, and whose nature is so sympathetically attuned to that of the artist that he understands him and finds delight in assisting the understanding of others. Swinburne had the truth of the matter in him when he said: "I have never been able to see what should attract men to the profession of criticism but the noble pleasure of praising." As seer, hierophant, and interpreter the critic performs an almost priestlike task. When criticism is inspired by the highest purpose, in which duty blends with privilege, one may even say of it, as has been said of love—"all other pleasures are not worth its pains."

The serious amateur who in the hearing of music feels a vague stirring as in the presence of something which itself is vague, desires more of the critic's discriminating power. He has heard that music is not only an art of expression but is also an art of form. It enters the soul through many channels. Hearing—as we use the term in respect to a piece of music—is a complex process. In the first place there is the physical consciousness of sounds of a particular pitch, timbre, and intensity. We may hear them as we hear the warble of a bird, the mutter of distant thunder, the sigh of the wind; no intellectual reaction need be involved, for these sounds may be unrelated and unorganized. Aside from possible chance associations, which one person may have and another may not, they are mere sense impressions which act in the same way upon people of higher and lower grades of culture. In the next stage, however, there are more refined and intricate processes involved. The tones are no longer detached and isolated, but are combined with one another by an act of will on the part of the composer. This coalescence into logical design, being an intellectual operation, demands an intellectual operation for its apprehension. The hearer perceives plan, system, order, unified variety. A third stage also appears: each tone or phrase is an emotional centre. The successions and combinations of tones are charged with a potency which their qualities as agreeable sensation and ingenious artifice cannot explain. There is a stirring of the spirit to unknown depths, the final cause of which eludes analysis, but is felt to have its roots where every active impulse toward beauty has its birth. This exaltation and purging of the soul by harmony is doubtless music's highest sanction. There is an experience here for which no other art furnishes an equivalent. Music's very mystery and intangibility is the essential condition of much of its peculiar power. Nevertheless an earnest mind cannot be satisfied with a pleasure, however pure and elevating, that quickly dissolves, leaving no residue to be worked over by the memory. If uninitiated he yet believes that there must be a host of beauties in the works of the masters which he does not perceive. With all his delight in music he confesses that he has no firm standard of judgment, that he makes little or no progress in the appreciation of great music because he is at the mercy of his temperament, his habitudes, his prejudices, and his mental and physical condition at the moment. He would make his musical experiences a means of genuine intellectual gain, developing a power of enjoyment that is active not passive, one that strengthens his faculties of perception and discrimination by means of an exercise that he can supervise and direct to satisfying ends.

The amateur, too long neglected, is beginning to understand his needs and make them known, and I have already shown that his Macedonian cry is reaching attentive ears. He has no wish to become a brilliant player or vocalist, or if he has, there is no place in his life for the long preparatory drudgery. Neither would he be reconciled to courses in harmony and counterpoint. But he does wish to cultivate his ear and his powers of judgment, to know what to listen for, to hear what musicians hear in a musical performance, to learn in what consist the factors that make good music, to know what his musical friends are talking about when they discuss the new men and the new movements, to bring Beethoven and Wagner and Chopin into the circle of his familiars along with Raphael and Rembrandt, Shakespeare and Milton, Thackeray and Tennyson,—in a word he wishes to make music also, along with books and pictures and all beautiful things, a means of enriching his inward life.

In the succeeding chapters I have undertaken to show what music as a fine art has to offer to the amateur who begins with nothing but the most rudimentary knowledge of the formal principles and psychologic conditions of art in general. An ordinary sensitiveness to musical impressions is all that is required for admission to the imaginary class that I proceed to form. Let no one misunderstand my purpose, and suppose that I attach supreme value to technicalities because I give so large a space to them. I do so simply because a casual acquaintance with technical principles and methods is necessary as a means to the higher end, and because that is the knowledge in which the amateur is most deficient. His little learning will not be to him a dangerous thing; he is not to be refused a taste because he cannot drink deep at the Pierian springs. He need not fear that he will lose any of the fine intoxication that was his before. He will no longer say that he cannot see the forest for the trees — he will see trees and forest both. He will learn to adjust his mind so that the beauties of detail will reach him as well as the glory of the whole. "The laboratories," says a French writer, "are crowded with retorts, flowers and leaves are dissected under the microscope. But nothing of all this has spoiled the graces of the springtime or the splendors of setting suns."

CHAPTER III

DEFINITE HEARING: THE PROBLEM OF FORM

In the discussions that are to follow I shall have in mind that class of music lovers known as amateurs or dilettanti, meaning thereby those who do not practice music as a profession, and have little or no expert knowledge. I am thinking of genuine music lovers, the people who compose the serious part of opera and concert audiences, who encourage music in the home and in society, who like to discuss music and wish to make it more familiar. This enlarged appreciation, I assume, is to be gained chiefly by the ear, for the music lovers for whom this book is written are not required to be masters of the art of reading music. Books and musical reviews in the daily, weekly, and monthly press they will find it for their interest to consult frequently, and some of the best books on different branches of the subject will be specified. Lectures on music they will sometimes attend. In fact, I shall have pretty constantly in my mind the worthy band of lecturers whose work in colleges, schools, clubs and other private circles has recently become an important item in our national educational machinery. In this department of musical instruction traditions are still to be established, for there are as many methods as there are teachers, and many of these methods are crude and incomplete. My purpose is partly to indicate my own conception of the nature and scope of the subject of musical criticism—the topics involved and their mutual relations, the action of musical works upon the ear and mind of the listener, the æsthetic principles concerned, and the various means by which musical enjoyment may be increased and rational judgment ensured. I shall consider the needs of the learner, the preparation of the teacher (so far as the teacher is allowed to appear within the horizon of this volume) and the materials available for both. No exact system of study is proposed, certainly not a complete one. Many things that such a book might properly contain will probably be omitted, either intentionally or inadvertently. I wish to be as discursive as my whim dictates. My temperament is that of an explorer rather than that of a surveyor, and an explorer is one who leaves much to be sought out by the next comer. Suggestion rather than an organized program is the writer's best service in such a case as this; his best hope that he may be able to persuade others to enter a fresh field by confirming out of his own discoveries the bright promise of its invitations.

In its simplest terms the question resolves itself into this: What and how must one hear in listening to music? In respect to the *what* a listener is in quite a different situation from that involved in the presence of any other art. A musical composition exists only as it is performed; it does not really live until it has known a second birth. Moreover, music is movement; it is contained in time and not in space. We may go to an art gallery and study a picture or a statue at leisure; we are not compelled to form a judgment until we have deliberately examined all the details and put them together in our consciousness. In the case of a literary work the reader may be as deliberate as the picture gazer. The obscurities of Browning or Henry James simply require closer attention and slower progress than the lucid phrases of Tennyson or Hardy; the reader need not go on until he has understood them. But the musical piece passes as on the wings of the wind; we cannot arrest it for the sake of a reinspection. Moreover music is harmony as well as rhythmic melody; in the simplest song with piano accompaniment there are several parts to follow at the same time, while in a symphony, or still more in an opera or oratorio, the abundance and complexity of simultaneous elements not only presuppose vast powers of analytic perception on the part of the human ear, but also seem determined to baffle them. The weakness of music in the opinion of many philosophers — if it be a weakness — consists not so much in the character of its impressions as in the difficulty on the part of the hearer of getting any clear impressions at all. Even the trained musician feels this whenever he goes to a concert. The musical piece is volatile, intangible, evasive; it comes out of silence and vanishes into the unknown again. We are tantalized by this flying tumult of sweet sounds. We suspect that in the flood of harmony there are numberless beauties that escape us. We long to put forth some faculty of seizure that may arrest this phantom and hold it until it gives up all its secrets. If the educated musician is often thus perplexed it is not strange that the untaught amateur, catching a random charm here and another there, despairs of getting a definite image and yields to the vague excitement of nerve stimulation, or perhaps to the nobler, but no less transient absorption in mystical imaginings, and tries to be content therewith.

It is evident that these impediments can be overcome only by the development of some faculty which will enable the hearer to apprehend the design of a musical work and perceive some logical necessity in its progress. If the different factors combine into an artistic whole which gives each of them its *raison d'être*—if the composer's purpose is fully revealed only when the work is grasped entire, as a unity—then it is plain that the casual, disconnected impressions of the average non-musician do not give him the satisfaction which the work is intended to afford. His attention must be directed toward elements and qualities which he has not hitherto perceived. An amount of technical knowledge must be acquired that is at least sufficient to enable him to discover what the work actually contains and the real significance of each part in the total effect. These factors, not being intuitively discerned, require demonstration, and the novice in matters of musical science gladly accepts the guidance of the expert.

One who undertakes to assist musically untrained people to a comprehension of the works of the great composers, finds it necessary to ask: What is the actual musical experience of one who has no technical knowledge of the art? What does one who knows nothing of musical science or the laws of musical expression actually get out of a concert, recital, or opera? What is the difference in respect to perception and mental reaction between the untaught music lover and the expert critic? It is not easy to find an answer to these questions. The musician may call upon his imagination for a reply, but there is not much satisfaction in this, for it is extremely difficult for him to project himself into the mental state of one who has formed none of the habits that have become a second nature to one who has spent years in familiar association with the practical side of the art. These two individuals inhabit different worlds. Features that are instantly perceived and appraised by the one are overlooked by the other. The adept cannot recall his days of musical innocence, and so he asks for testimony from his non-musical brother, since instruction presupposes some knowledge of the mental status of the pupil. Such information, however, the latter finds it very difficult to give, for how can one furnish a clear account of impressions which are in their very nature unclear and elusive?

Certain aspects of the non-musician's musical experience will always be a mystery to an investigator as well as to the subject himself. One very radical distinction, however, is plain, and that is to be found in the fact that the musician's hearing of music is definite, while that of the casual hearer is indefinite. The latter is aware of a number of simple perceptions which may be very delightful even in isolation, but they do not coalesce in his consciousness into the orderly groups and divisions which, in their relations of balance, contrast, and fulfilment, make up a complete work of art. Furthermore, not being conversant with the principles of musical organization, he cannot be in that attitude of intelligent expectation which the musician, by reason of his specialized knowledge, is able to assume. Hence he fails to notice a great many sounds which the musician perceives because he is more or less awake to their necessity in the tonal scheme. The musician's perception of sounds is reinforced by his acquaintance with the procedure of the art of composition, and he is thus able to hear each phrase as a preparation for that which is to come; his mind is alert, as if about to spring ahead of the actual tones and anticipate their direction, or at least he can connect each passage with what he has already heard and construct in his mind more or less extensive divisions of the work as he goes along. No musician can do this to such a degree as to seize every detail of a large and intricate composition at the first hearing; there is a certain consolation to the amateur in reading the cautious, non-committal estimates of the professional critics on the morning after a first performance of a new symphony. But the critic's training enables him to direct his mind along certain legalized thoroughfares and gather details together into related groups, while to one who listens without method the sounds come in heterogeneous confusion, distinguished, if distinguished at all, only in gleams and flashes playing upon a current of vague sonority.

The primary task of the ambitious music lover, therefore, will be to learn some of the secrets of musical construction, in order that his hearing may take on that quality of definiteness which lies at the basis of a true musical appreciation. "Music," says Edmund Gurney, "may be described as having a definite or indefinite character according as the *individuality* of what is presented is or is not perceived; according as the person does or does not grasp something which can be recognized as itself and nothing else when the presentation is repeated, and can be reproduced in memory, not as the mere knowledge of a past fact, but with some vital realization of the actual experience. It is, indeed, obviously natural that any matter presented to the higher senses should exhibit definite æsthetic character in proportion to the degree in which striking form is perceived in it. The mind naturally assimilates and makes completely its own that on which it has brought its own activity to bear, and activity of mind demands an order of some kind in the matter on which it works."

On this plain psychologic principle the learner must take his stand. His first business is to develop that faculty which seeks for a systematic connection among audible phenomena. Without design and order — parts possessing a value not in themselves alone but in their contribution to the development of the whole — there is no work of art. "A book," says Alphonse Daudet (and he would have used the same expression for any artwork) "— a book is an organism; if it has not its organs in place it dies, and its corpse is a scandal." As the sounds enter the listener's brain he must strive to organize them there as the composer organized their symbols, to build up a tonal structure in his consciousness, a structure distinct, symmetrical, self-supporting—not only that the whole beauty of the work may be manifest, but also that its presence may remain established in the memory as a secure possession. Every musician is aware that music is not a random string of vivid sensations passing over like the clouds which leave no wake. To his mind each phrase is a consequence of that which went before and the necessary antecedent of that which follows. Just as each word in a line of poetry is by itself alone meaningless, so it is only in their connections and relations that sounds acquire æsthetic value. A single tone may be delightful in its physical effect, but apart from its fellows it has no expression, no character.[1]

The musician's pleasure comes from an active exercise of the attention directed by anticipation and sustained by memory. He enjoys the evidences of skill, of difficulties overcome, of the triumph of the composer or performer over his defiant material, the beauty that lies in reasoned design, development, and proportion. The ignorant hearer, on the other hand, is the sport of unknown forces. The sounds at any moment drive out of his mind the sounds he heard the moment before. In an orchestral composition he catches the most decided tone colors, he is exhilarated with the grandeur of accumulated crescendos, the fierce rush of the prestos, the electric pulse of the rhythms, and is soothed by the contrasting murmur of soft melodies. He enjoys the brilliant execution of the pianist, the sympathetic voice of the famous singer. He is very conscious of melody—at least in fragments; he is less conscious of harmony; counterpoint is an unknown tongue. He is often like one who walks through a gallery of paintings, glancing from side to side, catching

[1] Exceptions to this principle, of course, occur in dramatic music, where, for example, a piercing high note, a fortissimo or harshly dissonant chord, or a distant trumpet tone will convey vivid suggestion by means of imitation or direct association.

glimpses of forms and colors, but when his excursion is over remembers little of what he has seen, and doubts if he is much the wiser for his experience. The musical world of the dilettante is often a sort of twilight region, in which everything is indistinct and many things beautiful are quite unseen.

Out of this misty realm of sensation the amateur, as soon as he is enlightened upon the real nature of art, wishes to emerge; he desires to arrange and solidify his impressions into something coherent, and fortify them with elements which he has not before perceived. In a word, he wishes to hear definitely instead of indefinitely.

In listening to a piece of music we observe the actual growth of an organic structure; we are witnesses of a process, each detail of which has a certain necessity in the realization of a design. A complete understanding of the work would imply an ability to comprehend not only the composer's ruling motive but also the function of every melodic and harmonic factor in the scheme. The question how a composer works becomes of interest. Many people seem to have the notion that a musical composition is of the nature of an improvisation, a succession of tones streaming out of a highly excited emotional condition. As regards a song—which in the case of a genius like Schubert may be struck out at a white heat and jotted down in a few feverish moments—this is in part true, but not so in respect to a work containing an abundance of varied ideas and elaborate in organization. Beethoven spent many days in writing the funeral march of the "Heroic" symphony, but we are not to suppose that his thoughts during that time were constantly fixed on mortality and the grave. We think of Tchaikovsky as a man in whom there was an especially direct connection between his moods and his music, but listen to what he says in one of his letters: "Those who imagine that a creative artist can, through the medium of his art, express his feelings at the moment when he is moved make the greatest mistake. Emotions, sad or joyful, can only be expressed retrospectively, so to speak. Without any special reason for rejoicing I may be moved by the most cheerful creative mood, and, *vice versa*, a work composed amid the happiest surroundings may be touched with dark and gloomy colors." We know that Beethoven and Chopin—composers whose music is charged to a high degree of emotional tension—were slow and laborious workers, Beethoven, particularly, being forced to struggle not only with the working out of his themes, but in many cases with the themes themselves, fairly twisting and hammering them into shape before he could begin to make use of them as constructive material. So true is it that a musical composition is a work of conscious reflective design that an actual personal emotion may even stand in the way of the best success in execution. Grieg's funeral march written in honor of his beloved friend, Rikard Nordraak, is on the whole rather commonplace, while thousands have been deeply moved by the pathos of "Ase's Death," written to suit a purely imaginary situation. The sublime "Dead March" in Handel's "Saul" and the awful dirge for Titurel in Wagner's "Parsifal" were certainly not inspired by personal experiences on the part of their authors. On the other hand, it would be impossible to find any connection between Mozart's distressing circumstances in 1788 and the three symphonies of that year—symphonies which seem fairly aglow with the *joie de vivre*. We need not regret that such is the case. It is the glory of art that its masterpieces are written in unconscious sympathy with universal human feeling, and are not the less sincere when they call forth tears such as their creators never shed.

In spite of this, I trust that I do not need to say that great music is something more than the result of a merely mechanical process. The truth seems to be that the first idea of the spirit and something of the form of a work often come in a sort of instantaneous vision, and the excited mood may often arise from an actual personal experience. The theme itself, which may suddenly flash upon the composer's mind, will often contain implicitly the essential character of the movement, as in the opening measures of Beethoven's Fifth symphony or the Scherzo of Mendelssohn's "Scotch" symphony. But the decision how the subject shall be treated and the giving of body and form to the idea is a very deliberate process; and when the composer takes pen in hand he must keep his head cool and call upon the result of his years of theoretical training, for his problem now is largely technical. This is even more the case with the composer, especially the instrumental composer, than it is with the sculptor or the painter, for his art is not at all imitative of nature, and so being free from any control by outward phenomena he is bound by the inner necessity of shaping his airy material by the laws which itself decrees.

It is these laws that the serious music lover wishes to understand, so far as a knowledge of them is necessary to enable him to follow a work in all its parts and take into his mind everything that contributes to its essential character. Order is heaven's first law in art as in nature, and the recognition of orderly arrangement in sounds is the first condition of definite impressions in hearing music. Even if the human mind does not instinctively seek for orderly relations among audible phenomena, at any rate a sense of these relationships and a desire for them can easily be awakened. It is a faculty to be cultivated like any other; it is a question of degrees. The craving for system and proportion is betrayed in the simplest folk song, even in the barren repetitions that abound in the music of savages. From such naïve devices up to the first movement of the "Heroic" symphony we find in every stage of musical progress the same necessity at work. A musical composition, like a drama or any other product of artistic contrivance, is a community in which each member ministers to the welfare of the whole, and draws from the whole organism the vital force which maintains its own existence. Says Dr. William Pole: "One may fancy a musical composition which, though it may be divided into measures and groups of measures, consists of a constant succession of heterogeneous ideas, none of which have any relation to any others going before or after them. This may be called amorphous music, that is, music without form; and even though the ideas presented might be very good, it would be tiresome and wearying to listen to. All great composers have perceived this, and they have, therefore, taken care to lighten the effort by causing a composition to contain but few novel ideas, and giving the chief interest by their skilful and musicianlike treatment."

The only fault that might be found with this statement is in the implied reason for this procedure on the part of composers; it is not to make things easy for the listener, but in obedience to an artistic necessity, that regularity of structure has prevailed. Even the classic forms of fugue and sonata, which Dr. Pole evidently has in mind, although their supremacy has long since passed, contain a principle that has never yet been abrogated. The leadership of certain themes and tonalities and the return to them after other melodies and keys have intervened is still the method by which a straggling incoherence is avoided, and consistency, coherence, and unity maintained. "All things," says Thoreau, "are subjected to a rotary motion, either gradual and partial, or rapid and complete, from the planet and system to the simplest shellfish and pebbles on the beach. As if beauty resulted from an object's turning on its axis, or from the turning of others about it." In musical organisms, from the lowest to the highest, we find application of the universal law of rhythm — we find action and reaction, control and subordination, growth from the simple to the complex, adjustment of elements for the attainment of order, unity, and reasoned progress.

The sum of the matter is that a musical work, whatever its dimensions, however various and affluent in ideas, however copious in emotional change and contrast, must still, from the most liberal point of view, possess consistency; everything must tend to an impression to which all the parts contribute; so that when surveyed in its entirety it will appear that it is one thing and not many things. Like an organism in the natural world, all the parts draw their nourishment from the common current of life, and in turn give that life the means of fulfilling the destiny which it was intended to serve in its own special kingdom.

William F. Apthorp, in an interesting little essay on *The Non-musician's Enjoyment of Music,* cites the case of a concert goer who received no intelligible impression from orchestral music, all instrumental music being equally meaningless to him, but who intensely enjoyed Brahms's C minor symphony, while Schumann's symphony in D minor left him indifferent, and he asks the reader to explain this anomaly. But Mr. Apthorp's paradox, as he states it, is impossible — the person in question must have obtained some kind of definite impression from the Brahms symphony, else he would not have preferred it to the other. There must have been something more perceived than mere "volume, dynamic force, energy." We speak of the hearing of musically ignorant people as vague, but it is never entirely vague. From even the most bewildering orchestral complexity of a Strauss or a Reger there will emerge bits of melody, rhythm, and tone color that will convey notions of something salient and individual. Hence the music lover who wishes to increase his enjoyment does not need to be provided with a new faculty — he needs only to be shown how to develop the powers of perception and coördination which he already possesses and to employ them as the very conditions of musical art demand.

"It is clear," says Miss Ethel Puffer, "that the real musical beauty is in the melodic idea; in the sequence of tones which are indissolubly one, which are felt together, one of which cannot exist without the other. Musical beauty is in the intrinsic musical form. . . . The perfect structure will be such a unity that it will be felt as one. . . . The ideal musical consciousness would have an ideally great range; it not only realizes the concatenation [of harmonies and keys], but it would take it in as one takes in a single phrase, a simple tune, retaining it from first note to last. The ordinary musical consciousness has merely a much shorter breath. It can 'feel' an air, a movement; it cannot feel a symphony, it can only perceive the relation of keys and harmonies therein. With repeated hearing, study, experience, this span of beauty may be indefinitely extended — in the individual, as in the race. But no one will deny that the direct experience of beauty, the single æsthetic thrill, is measured exactly by the length of this span. It is only genius — hearer or composer — who can operate *à longue haleine.*"

The early lessons in the noble art of listening to music must, therefore, deal much with matters of form and structure. For two reasons — first for the sake of making the hearing definite and complete, and second for the pleasure derived from the ability to recognize the composer's skill in handling the devices that make for artistic perfection. Even though the scientific elements in art are agencies to higher ends, nevertheless, since they are a *sine qua non*, a full appreciation of art is not possible without some knowledge of their functions, and the ability to appraise them. The parts which are welded together by the composer's craft are not only beautiful in themselves but still more beautiful in their relations of mutual service. Many people who praise music rapturously miss this great distinctive element, without which there is, properly speaking, no art. What they lose is not only valuable in respect to immediate impression but necessary to make the impression permanent. As I have already said, a dim recollection of emotional states is not sufficient for one who desires that art should contribute to the riches of the intellectual life. One longs for a concrete image that can be retained, reviewed, and recognized at a later appearance, and the condition of this objective reality lies not in memories of pleasant excitement, nor even in memories of harmonic and orchestral color, but in memories of form. Form is not only an indispensable means by which the artist makes clear to himself and communicates to others the impulse that stirred his soul to utterance, but it is in itself a thing to be admired by reason of the beauty that lies in proportion, order, and unified variety. The random hearer of music, like the nonchalant stroller in cathedral aisles, perceives the variety but not the unity. He is not drawn by the intellectual strength that controls the rebellious forces which the artist wields. There is an inexhaustible delight in following the artist's plan as he develops his motives, builds up his designs, and adjusts his melodies, rhythms, and harmonies into patterns of grace and symmetry.

In no art can this factor be omitted by the dilettante. In every good painting the artist selects, rejects, and arranges; never does he give a literal photographic reproduction of his subject. Straight lines and curves echo or supplement one another; objects balance and relieve one another; masses, colors, lights and shades are arranged for the purpose of variety, reinforcement, and concentration; the observer's eye is directed by a multitude of subtle expedients to the central point of interest. Even in literature the same principle holds good. The casual reader who studies Professor Richard G. Moulton's *Shakespeare as a Dramatic Artist* and Professor Bliss Perry's *Art of Fiction* will have his eyes opened to the importance of form and arrangement even in those departments of art where the author had seemed most free to follow nature unrestrained.

When listening to music is active and not passive there are two mental operations involved, viz., expectation and recollection. One reason, doubtless, why a musical work that is worthy of repetition is more enjoyed at subsequent hearings than at the first is because these two faculties are more and more alive. Not only is expectation aroused from moment to moment, but expectation is satisfied, giving the pleasure that is at the bottom of a large share of our mental and physical enjoyments—that of relief following a sense of effort. Memory, becoming more exact while at the same time it reaches over a larger surface, retains impressions of beauty when sounds have ceased, and joins them in reinforcement to beauties present and to come.

In the music lover's initiation into the mysteries of structure he will make trial of the simpler and more regular forms first, and that means, of course, the so-called classic forms. To plunge into the complexities of Wagner and the subtleties of Debussy before one is able to trace the design of a Mendelssohn "Song without Words" would result only in mental confusion. The commonplace rules of all education are sufficient guides. The classic forms and diatonic harmonies are to be chosen at the beginning because they are the basis of modern musical structure, and the study of them clears away from the student's mind those difficulties that are greatest because they are fundamental. The first chapters in the book of form will, therefore, deal with the song form, the sonata, the rondo, the variation, and the fugue.

The study of form may for convenience be divided into two departments, viz., rhythmic structure and thematic development. For the sake of clearness it seems best to me to transfer the consideration of the first to the chapter on melody and rhythm, simply premising that the logical method in instruction would be to exercise the learner in the recognition of the fundamental metrical structure of section, phrase, and period as the basis of order in the variety of rhythmic figuration, before he makes acquaintance with the larger specialized forms, rhythmic arrangement being primary and universal in music, thematic alteration being derived and secondary.

In the more highly organized musical compositions the variation of theme constitutes the device whose happy discovery, together with the principle of repetition and relativity in tonality and rhythm, gave to musical architecture its symmetry, unity of design, and stability. Its importance has been variable. The classic masters were content with a few themes, and concentrated their effort on the modification and combination of these, while the invention of a lavish profusion of novel ideas has been more consciously the aim of the romantic composers. Nevertheless, the subjection of themes to ever-changing aspects of shape and color, and the dominance of certain tonalities, have always been held as the chief means by which musical invention is to be restrained from falling into a license and disorder that would defeat its own purpose. The listener, therefore, must hold in his mind the thought of organized development as he follows a performance phrase by phrase. He must know something of the possibilities that lie in thematic work, the processes employed by the masters in the evolution of movements out of the leading themes and motives. "An exact survey of the nature and means of the art of thematic construction," says Arrey von Dommer, "can be obtained by any one who can read notes or play the piano to some extent. Whoever accustoms himself to study music from this point of view will in a short time obtain from any composition a far higher enjoyment. He who considers the matter earnestly will perceive an organic life where before he was conscious only of details, indistinct outlines, detached fragments of melody, rhythm, or harmony. To hear music correctly and with intelligence, to perceive and comprehend a musical composition as a work of art developed organically out of an idea, must always be the effort of the music lover. To accomplish this one must have far more than the ability to be agreeably excited by musical sounds. Where one person is satisfied with a mere superficial pleasure and a comfortable feeling of idle reverie, perceiving nothing but a mere hazy and uncertain succession of tone pictures, the expert musician sees a fulness of animated forms, proceeding from one another and flowing into one another, all closely united by a firm spiritual tie. The artificial enthusiasm, or the hardly concealed indifference, which one often observes in concert halls, even in the performance of masterpieces, shows plainly enough how superficially in most cases music is heard, and that in such instances there is a complete absence of any real love of the art. Where one finds himself falling into this, there must by all means be an effort to come into a closer understanding of the subject. The study of the development of themes and phrases is the first condition of a true art understanding; besides that, it is an inexhaustible source of constantly renewed enjoyment."

The only amendment that should be made to this very satisfactory statement is that even one who cannot read notes or play the piano need not be shut out from the privilege of recognizing themes and following them in their chameleon-like changes. A few repetitions of themes will enable the ear to hold them by their salient features, and with experience there will be constant growth in the power of systematic observation.

At this point it is time to bring in a qualification. It is very easy to overdo the matter in expounding musical analysis, and use it as a means of suppressing imagination and chilling emotion. Form, structure, harmony, and counterpoint are to be explained only so far as a knowledge of their laws is useful for the training of the observation and confirming the power to appreciate æsthetic unity. The novice need not know an inversion from a suspension; double counterpoint need not be even a name to him; these things are no more required for the enjoyment of music than a familiarity with metrical terminology is needed for the enjoyment of poetry. The essential thing is to *hear* the subtle accents and shades in verse melody, to *hear* everything that goes on in a fine piece of music, not to label and classify scientific devices. Many teachers are so enamored with the theoretical side of their art that they carry the dissection of form to a superfluous excess and encourage pedantry rather than real æsthetic perception. The instructor will often find among his disciples prosaic natures who readily acquire a lively interest in the mechanical construction of musical compositions; they love to see the "wheels go 'round"; whether a work is beautiful or not is a minor consideration, provided it furnishes them an opportunity for gratifying their morbid passion for analysis. Such are to be found in a certain class of Wagner enthusiasts, who are so busy in identifying the "leading motives" which they have found in the "guides" that they are often cold to the splendor and passion of the music. On the other hand there are musical devotees, for whom we should cherish respect, who revolt at this whole process of vivisection. The dry exposition of subject and counter-subject, of phrase and period, of link passage and codetta, is an offence to them. They heap contumely upon the "analytical program." They shout amen to the opinion of Debussy who, as Mrs. Liebich tells us, introduced his salutatory as musical critic of the *Revue blanche* with the announcement that he should endeavor to trace in a musical work "the many different emotions which have helped to give it birth, and also to demonstrate its inner life. This will surely be accounted of greater interest than the game which consists in dissecting it as if it were a curious timepiece. Men in general forget that as children they were forbidden to dismember their playthings, but they still persist in poking their æsthetic noses where they are not wanted." Felix Weingartner points out a danger from the excessive study of treatises on form and analytic program books, when he says: "As we are trained by reading program books and guides to hear and look at the works not in their entirety but in detail, it is only the small minority who, on hearing a new composition, consider the general impression of the whole before commencing to consider the details; yet these latter can only be comprehensible by and in view of the *ensemble*."

The answer to these objections has been given in the preceding pages. The wisdom of the warning must, however, be acknowledged and the saving doctrine found between the two extremes. On the whole it may be said that the dangers that lie in the emphasis upon technicalities are less than the dangers of ignorance. It is with art as it is with nature — the lore of birds and plants and trees need not check but may stimulate the sense of beauty and the ardor of mystical companionship. The most impassioned writers on nature, the most eloquent, the most alive to the broad aspects and the poetic suggestions, are the men of scientific knowledge, with powers accustomed to minute observation. The discriminating vision, certainly, is not sufficient alone; there must be the large synthesis and the impulsive joy. Not every botanist would be an acceptable walking companion for Wordsworth or Hazlitt. When observation has done its work and the sight is cleared, one asks for "that undisturbed silence of the heart which alone is perfect eloquence." The learning of the laboratory may miss the last secret. The rich and rare combination is that of the naturalist's eye and the poet's soul.

This development of the analytic and the synthetic powers in coöperation is one of the finest gains of the study of musical form. This appreciation of form, it must be emphatically observed, should be as liberal and elastic as form itself has proved to be in the evolution of modern music. The classic patterns of sonata, rondo, and fugue served a necessary, an inevitable purpose in the progressive upbuilding of musical art, and the works of Bach, Mozart, and Beethoven stand in monumental dignity for the admiration of all coming generations. But in the fulness of time these forms, having served their end, tend to loosen, expand, and disintegrate; the elements of which they are composed — the phrase and the period — readjust themselves into other schemes of design. The later tendency has been to proceed from strict form to free form. The composer is no longer bound to adhere to an authoritative model, which was devised when the development of strict form was the supreme requirement for artistic advancement. This technical mastery is at last attained and the composer now makes expression his supreme end, the feeling and the contrast of feeling determining the form, regular or irregular, according to the wilfulness of the moment. This emancipation of the art from the restraints of strict form has been especially manifest in vocal music. Wagner has shown us with admirable clearness in *The Music of the Future* and in *Actor and Singer* how the aria form, which had become standardized in the opera, forbade a free development of a continuous dramatic idea by breaking up a scene into a number of isolated fragments which he calls "tunes," consisting of two or three symmetrical divisions, and separated by dry recitatives. Under this plan the action could move only by fits and starts, and no large and comprehensive scheme of poetic development was possible. It was as if Shakespeare had been compelled to write the speeches of his characters each in a prescribed number of lines and place them at regular distances apart. Nothing less could content Wagner than "turning the whole full stream to which Beethoven swelled German music into the channel of the musical drama." By this he meant not Beethoven's sonata form and proportionally measured periods, but the richness, the unlimited abundance, the continuous flow of the Beethoven music, where there was no "framing of a melody," no padding with conventional passage work, but where "everything became melody." Wagner's form is a form that is not molded by any mechanical pattern, but one that grows directly out of the buoyant expansive impulse that inspires the poetry and the action. Each situation, each line even, has its own individual movement. The form is completely free.

The same tendency is seen in the song, from Schubert to Hugo Wolf. In such a song as "Who is Sylvia?" or "Leise fliehen (The Serenade)" the melodic form is conventional and would be as well suited to many other poems. But in "The Phantom Double" and "Death and the Maiden," many of the songs of Schumann, most of the songs of

Grieg and Strauss, perhaps all of the songs of Wolf, the form of each melody belongs to the particular poem to which it is set and to no other. The form is free, irregular so far as musical design is concerned. And the hearer must perforce listen to the music from the standpoint of the words, and the form beauty is not one of space proportions or a circle of tonalities, but a beauty of adaptation.

This principle has been carried over to that department of instrumental music known as "representative" or "illustrative" music. A subject like Liszt's "Preludes" or Strauss's "Death and Glorification"—a subject that has literary or pictorial progress and conclusion—cannot follow any one of the orthodox schemes of design. As a whole and in details the music must issue from the poetic idea and imagery. The form is free, and there may be as many forms as there are program symphonies or symphonic poems.

In abstract instrumental music also this emancipating impulse has been felt. In such works as Tchaikovsky's last symphony and Chopin's Ballades and Fantaisies the composer is as unshackled in the shaping of the entire outline as he is in the invention of his melodies. The themes may or may not "develop" according to the classic method. It is of no consequence where they are repeated or whether they are repeated at all. In succession of keys, in balance of rhythmic figures, the composer is constrained by no outward pressure of custom, but only by an inner compulsion which bids him put his emotion into a form which will give that emotion an unimpeded outlet.

There is a class of critics at the present day, including some of our ablest writers, who joyfully hail these later tendencies as a sign of the abrogation of the formal principle, as the triumph of feeling over convention, the close approach to ultimate truth. But these writers hardly mean all that they seem to say. The adaptation of parts to a common aim is the very condition of life in art; without unification of plan art dies, for incoherence is the negation of art. Their protest is actually directed against the despotic subjection of art to certain standardized types of form. Even in Wagner's dramas and Elgar's oratorios and Debussy's tone-poems, with their unrestrained pliancy and power of instantaneous adjustment to thought and situation, there is no violation of the supreme law, liberally interpreted. Forms change but form remains.

Form in the bolder practice of the present day grows from within outward. It is plastic, is not bound to imitate an academic model, but is shaped to the special needs of the subject or motive, finding its sole business to bring that to expression by whatever novelty of device is most efficient. The music lover, training himself to recognize and follow musical structure as a development out of certain germ ideas, must also recognize in every case the purpose for which the form exists, whether this form be strict or free. The error of the opponents of Liszt and Wagner consisted in setting up certain necessary and admirable forms as infallible and immutable standards; it was the error of those in all times who have opposed freedom in art because they could not see that form is a means and not an end. Formlessness indeed is fatal; but at the same time the oonception of what constitutes proper form must be left to those who create, and must be allowed to obey and not to control invention. As "the thoughts of men are widened with the process of the suns," so old modes and fashions of expression are left behind. Forms live and grow because the spirit grows. Three hundred years ago Edmund Spenser, in his *Hymne in Honour of Beautie*, uttered what comes near to the central truth of art:

> "So every spirit, as it is most pure,
> And hath in it the more of heavenly light,
> So it the fairer bodie doth procure
> To habit in, and it more fairely dight
> With chearefull grace and amiable sight;
> For of the soule the bodie form doth take;
> For soule is form and doth the bodie make."

CHAPTER IV

THE BEAUTY OF MELODY AND RHYTHM

In the foregoing discussion the word form has been used rather vaguely, for my purpose is to study the action of music upon the mind of the music lover so far as it has to do with his immediate enjoyment, and not to draw up a treatise on the scientific materials of music which would pass muster before an examining board of theorists. In speaking of form I have had in mind what Gurney calls "the individualizing element, the element by which things are known and recognized." Form—melodic, harmonic, or rhythmic—is that which imparts a notion of plan, order, consistency, organization among successions either of single tones or masses of tones. Whether under such a designation as "sonata form" including the whole compass of a composition, or the contour of a component as small as a single motive, or a chord combination that establishes a definite tonality or group of tonalities—form consists in any arrangement of auditory images which gives the notion of something individual and self-consistent. The recognition of design and unity amid variety is, as I have tried to show, the prime condition of the appreciation of a musical composition as a work of art. On this basis we can discuss a composition with our neighbor, confident that we have both received impressions that are sufficiently definite to permit comparison of opinions.

Among the components of musical effect melody seems to claim the first consideration, for whatever may be said of the sensuous charm and expressional value of harmony and tone color, it is certain that the fundamental musical consciousness is that of progression from point to point, with the rhythmic melodic outline as the essential agency that binds the whole together into a coherent self-supporting entity. Rhythmic accent is doubtless still more fundamental as mere sense impression, but as beats of varying degrees of force, or periodic variations of tone lengths, do not in themselves produce a musical outline without a perception of definite changes of pitch, the impression of tunefulness, with a more or less apparent rhythmic distribution, is the prime source of the average musical experience. Both taught and untaught music lovers are more distinctly aware of rhythmic melody in the first hearing of a piece than of any other feature, and among the untaught hearers nine out of ten are distinctly observant of nothing else, except, perhaps, certain dynamic and color effects in performance. That one passage is louder than another, or that a piccolo shrieks or a kettle-drum rumbles, would, of course, be noticed even by a child; but it could hardly be said that intelligence is at work in such an observation. When the mind is able to put impressions together in orderly relations, it is melody first of all that awakens the joyful sense of beauty.

Since the consciousness of melody seems to be so nearly instinctive and universal, the question naturally arises, Can an appreciation of melody be increased by instruction? If by this is meant, Can a love of *good* melody be awakened by technical explanations; can the points of superiority in certain melodies be pointed out in such a way that general principles can be deduced to serve as infallible tests for melody in general, the answer must be negative. If a listener does not feel in his heart that Schubert's "Who is Sylvia?" or the theme of the Larghetto of Beethoven's Second symphony is not a better tune than the latest popular song that came last week and will be forgotten to-morrow, there is no possible way of convincing him. We may tell him that a fine tune has individual character, a sort of positiveness that distinguishes it from others and takes firm hold upon the memory, and he will ask us if "Yankee Doodle" does not meet these conditions. If my friend asserts that "Pop goes the Weasel" is a better tune than Wolfram's "Invocation" I may assert the contrary; but my assertion is purely dogmatic, and I may have no recourse at last except to call him hard names. The only method of bringing the Philistine to a better mind would be to give him a course in themes by the great masters if he would submit to the discipline, and if he inquired why we made these particular selections we should be obliged to fall back on the general consent of the musical world as our warrant. To so slight a degree does anything like established law reign in matters of melody that we are sometimes almost provoked to say that a taste in tunes is as irresponsible as a preference in salads or millinery.

Standards of good and bad in melody we feel that there must be, but when we try to draw conclusions that will serve as laws we find decisions of equally intelligent arbiters varying with periods, nationalities, customs, and temperaments. There are melodies, to use Hanslick's expression, which "once were beautiful"; and we may also believe that there are melodies, now friendless, that sometime will be beloved. When "Tannhäuser" first appeared, the stock accusation against it on the part of many professional musicians and critics was that it had no melody. The same charge was at one time brought against Gounod's "Faust," although to many this will seem incredible. At the first performance of Beethoven's "Fidelio" in one of the Italian cities, an indignant hearer called out, "That isn't music, that's philosophy." Wagner is now recognized as a great melodist, but many ardent Wagnerians deny the melodic gift to Strauss and Debussy. They may be correct in this, but in view of past instances a cautious man would hesitate in putting himself on record with such an affirmation. Many lovers of Beethoven, Schubert, and Chopin do not find melody in the organ and piano works of Sebastian Bach, while to the Bach disciple these works are flooded with melody of a high order of beauty. The precisely opposite effects of Liszt's melody on different critics are well known. Even the fact of spontaneity and originality, which would seem at first thought easy to determine, is constantly in dispute.

The explanation of many of these anomalies and others similar to them is to be found in habit. The well-known maxim, *omne ignotum pro magnifico,* does not apply to popular musical taste. Melody has undergone progressive changes, especially during the past century, and where melody is not recognized in a new work the explanation will commonly be found in the fact that the themes are unlike those to which the listeners have been accustomed. When composers such as Wagner and Schubert have failed to win approval at the outset the trouble has lain in the novelty of their melodic forms. The difficulty with the average man to-day is very much what it was with many cultivated musicians when "Tannhäuser" and "Lohengrin" were first performed—he accepts as melody only those successions of tones in which there is a decided accent at equal distances, and in which the rhythmic phrases that result are so few and so evenly balanced that the mind can follow the simple design with the minimum of effort, and hence easily receives the impression of something distinct and complete. These brief melodic forms, which writers nowadays, following Wagner's appellation, call "tunes" or "dance tunes" to distinguish them from melody in which this simple mathematical proportion is avoided, are based on the more fundamental harmonic relations, with regularly returning cadences and half cadences. No disparagement is implied in this classification, for among these rhythmically square-cut tunes we find some of the finest inspirations of musical genius. Hymn tunes are of this character, also folk songs, countless themes of surpassing beauty by Mozart, Beethoven, Handel, Schubert, Verdi, and all the great masters of song—melodies which the world has taken into its heart of hearts as a treasure incomparably precious. No training is required to appreciate these, but a restriction to them on the part of the average man forbids him to follow the broader flights to which melody, especially in the latter time, has adventured. Mark Twain, after hearing "Lohengrin," declared that there was only one good tune in the whole opera, meaning, of course, the "Bridal Chorus." It was not that each phrase in this melody would have seemed to him actually more beautiful than many other phrases in the work if an equally distinct impression could have been received; but here was something terse, brief, and regular, the whole thing hung together, it was grasped and retained in consciousness as something distinct and tangible. Another hearer would find satisfying melody in the king's prayer and

Elsa's appeal, but little or none in the first part of the second act. To many listeners the last act of "The Mastersingers" is a rather monotonous plain diversified by a few melodious outcroppings, such as Walther's "Prize Song," the Quintet and the "Mastersingers' March"; while in "Tristan and Isolde" no such salient points of vantage are to be found. The question here is not of good or poor melody, but the ability to recognize any melodic contour at all.

Whatever may be said of the possibility of developing taste in melody, it will not be denied, I think, that one persistent aim on the part of the immature music lover should be to develop the power of apprehension beyond the confines of the "tune" into those regions where the great composers have found the amplest melodic freedom. The hearer must be practiced in following the melodic bounding line over larger and larger spaces. At the same time the unequal divisions, all the elevations and subsidences whose variety and abundance seem at first to disappoint the instinctive demand for unity, must be perceived as essential items in the design. It is only a question of extending the mental embrace to enfold larger and larger and more and more intricate patterns. One takes for the starting point a short and symmetrical form, such as Brahms's "Slumber Song" or MacDowell's "To a Wild Rose"; the next step reaches a form that is larger but without rhythmic diversity, such as Schubert's

"Wohin?" or the F major Étude in Chopin's Op. 25; then to "through-composed" songs of Schubert, Schumann, or Strauss, the selections systematically varying in extent and changefulness of structure. The release of the mind from bondage to the four-measure and eight-measure ratio in metrical division means complete emancipation of the music lover in his appreciation of melody. He can now range freely in the newly discovered regions which modern music has conquered. In the vast serpentine line of Wagner's *melos* there is a titanic shaping power at work amid all the apparent melodic confusion; just as in the magnificent sky line of the Adirondacks seen from the hills beyond Lake Champlain there is balanced strength and symmetry in the seemingly irregular sweep of the majestic curves.

That this expansion of the powers of observation will be followed by an increase of taste in the matter of sheer melodic quality cannot be positively asserted, but it seems reasonable to suppose that it must be so. A hearer who has trained his mind to follow all the sinuous windings of the tone stream in a fugue by Bach, a symphony movement by Tchaikovsky, or an act in a Wagner drama, joyfully yielding his mind to every ebb and swell because he realizes that the highest ends of artistic expression are answered by this tidal motion, will surely not fail to catch the beauty of the tuneful phrases which are involved at every turn. A new conception of melody will be his, one that will by no means deprive him of his old delight in melody of the simpler forms.

The secret of the ability to follow all the fluctuations of melodic outline and to grasp the multifarious changes of structure, lies in the cultivation of the sense of rhythm. Music, "the ideal motion," consists of a succession of moments filled by sound, and the gratification that comes to the hearer depends for its intensity very much upon his consciousness that the tones and phrases are swayed by some law of order. Everywhere in the universe rhythm persists; wherever there is life there is ebb and flow, action and reaction, oscillation, vibration, compensating forces that support and relieve one another, giving to the observer as he surveys them an impression of ease combined with power. If we mystically interpret music as symbolic of the inner life of the universe, it is by virtue of its rhythmic motion.

It is the opinion of many scholars that rhythm precedes melody in historic sequence, that among the lower races pleasure in the production of tones in regular beats is more primitive than the desire for changes in pitch. Says Richard Wallaschek: "Rhythm, taken in a general sense to include keeping in time, is the essence in music, in its simplest form as well as in the most skilfully elaborated fugues of modern composers. To recall a tune the rhythm must be revived first, and the melody will easily be recalled. Completely to understand a musical work ceases to be difficult when once its rhythmical arrangement is mastered; and it is through rhythmical performance and rhythmical susceptibility that musical effects are produced and perceived. From these several data I conclude that the origin of music must be sought in a rhythmical impulse in man."

In this dependence upon division of time for intelligibility music conforms to the great law of proportion by which all art is sustained—proportion in space in architecture, painting, and sculpture, proportion in time in poetry and the dance. Richard Watson Gilder sings:

> "No poet he who knows not the great joy
> That pulses in the flow and rush of rhythm;
> Rhythm, which is the seed and life of life,
> And of all art the root and branch and bloom."

In music the marked differences of taste and comprehension among people otherwise of equal intelligence is chiefly due (where tone-deafness does not exist) to the disparities in the ability to perceive order and plan. People say, for instance, that they do not "understand" such and such musical compositions. They mean by this that the mind does not adjust itself to the rhythmic plan of the music, that the combinations are too intricate and changeable to be apprehended as definite coherent form, and a sense of bewilderment ensues which is fatal to pleasure. No one ever professes inability to understand a simple dance or a march. One may not like it for any reason or no reason, but it will be easy to follow in its rhythmic arrangement and therefore intelligible. Unity without variety is as unsatisfying, in a different way, as variety without unity. One reason of the dislike for dances or marches which many feel may be the monotony of the reiteration of strong beats, a perception of regularity that is agreeable at first becoming annoying, because the nerve centres affected are soon wearied by the persistent attack upon them. It is evident that the full degree of pleasure is derived when there is variety enough to keep the expectation constantly alive, and a clear enough accomplishment of unity to give an impression of reason and order in the result.

The experiences of the individual in his contact with ever-increasing variety and freedom of rhythmic design is paralleled by the experience of the race. Composers who have pushed the art of music onward have done so by enlarging their resources of rhythm and producing works which were beyond the ability of most of their contemporaries to grasp with intelligent satisfaction. It has been writers like Mendelssohn, who did not put any new burden upon the rhythmic appreciative faculty, who have been at once understood and approved.

The first business, therefore, of the lover of music who wishes to keep pace with the progress of the art and open his mind to the beauties that meet him in the works of the best composers, is to strengthen his ability to comprehend complex rhythmic relations. He will find that there are certain tone patterns that are uniform in their regularity and very obvious in their reiteration of a few simple figures. The "tunes," which were spoken of in an earlier part of this chapter, are of this class, as well as all passages in which a dancelike movement is given by means of sharp accents recurring at short intervals. It requires no education to recognize and follow these persistent beats and parallel phrases—nothing but the ability to keep step in a march or to beat time uniformly to a dance. As music becomes more highly organized these simple rudimentary forms give way to freer forms, and the listener whose rhythmic reactions are narrowly limited finds himself utterly confused by the complex tone patterns which, in their displacement of accents, avoidance of cadences, their interweaving of melodic lines and harmonic masses, their cross currents and eddies of shifting tones, seem to avoid every semblance of order and system. And yet it is only a difference of degree. Unity and plan are there as well as in the rudimentary figures that are so gratifying to the beginner's elementary perceptions. He must simply go to work, with the assistance of some one more adept in these mysteries, to learn the method by which these puzzling combinations resolve into coherence and symmetry.

The first glance at an elaborate musical score seems to offer to the neophyte a spectacle of heterogeneous confusion, for if he marks off with his eye the little compartments within the perpendicular bar-lines he discovers a bewildering diversity in the appearance of their contents. A keen listening, however, reveals to him that within this profusion of "sounding arabesques" there are distinct pulses or beats which appear to supply the need of an underlying system of order. In marches, waltzes, and in a multitude of compositions beside, these beats are very aggressive and are followed without much strain upon the attention; in other works, such as fugues, many forms of church music, long sections of Wagner's dramas, the solid bony framework, if we may use such a comparison, is dissolved in a fluid, seemingly shapeless progression of sounds. Nevertheless, in all instrumental compositions and the vast majority of vocal pieces, the mass of sound—twisting, twining, condensing, expanding into every variety of tone outline—rests firmly upon a steady support of beats and simple measure combinations, and the recognition of the underlying principle of order gives to the hearer the happy intimation that within the flood of music there is definiteness and reason. Just as the profusion of ornament upon capitals, architraves, friezes, and cornices rests upon columns or arches standing at equal distances from one another, so in music the multifarious forms of rhythmic figuration are saved from incoherence by the throb of the steady pulses within. Or we may compare the arrangement to curves or waves, the basic or typical curves, which are regular, being overlaid by other curves which are free to take any length, to interlace, even at times to interfere with one another. Comparisons are more or less confusing, but analysis shows that in music are united two rhythmic conceptions—one, which we may call the figuration, giving variety, the other, which we may call the metre, giving simplicity, definiteness of structure, and regularity. The unit of metre is the measure, corresponding in a general way to the foot in verse. The measure is either double or triple in respect to its accent scheme, these fundamental accents occurring at intervals of two, three, or four beats, as indicated by the measure sign—$\frac{2}{4}$, $\frac{3}{4}$, $\frac{6}{8}$, etc. The measure units are themselves combined into distinct groups known as sections, phrases, and periods, the points of separation and union among them being made apparent to the ear by melodic and harmonic means (known to theorists as cadences, half cadences, interrupted cadences, and the like) which give the impression of little points of rest to which the music strives, only to take a new leap in its career; or else, still oftener, points where this expectation of a subsidence of movement is disappointed, this expectation nevertheless affording a definite point of support for the attention. The normal arrangement of measures which form the sustaining arches of the tone edifice, is in groups of fours, eights, and sixteens. This standard plan is frequently modified, and the eight and sixteen measure outline gives way to divisions of six, nine, twelve, and other irregular successions. Even where the multiple of four is retained, the composer loves to evade the formality of the plan by harmonic and rhythmic devices that keep the attention poised over longer curves. A large amount of metrical freedom is allowed the composer, but only on the condition that he shall not abuse the privilege and violate the law of balance and proportion.

It is the comparatively simple metrical order, therefore, on which the hearer must base his attention. He must feel the metrical pulse beating in the veins of his own musical consciousness, and from out the tangle of harmonies, melodies, and ornamentation there will emerge the firm outline of a design which makes everything coherent, and gratifies that innate sense of order which governs the instinctive human activities and is also the ruling principle of art.

The failure mentally to accompany the rhythmic progress of a piece of music is often due, not to a congenital lack of rhythmic faculty, but to the distraction of the attention from the characteristic beat and metrical divisions by other elements which are for the moment more engaging—brilliant passage work, perhaps, or glaring tone color. The last of the merits in good piano playing to be appreciated by the average listener is the phrasing; but phrasing is simply making the rhythmic structure apparent to the ear. First a general knowledge of the foundation principles of musical design in distribution of metrical accents and groups of accents, then the attention which sets in motion analogous beats and waves in the consciousness, and the listener will soon find a new world of pleasure opening within him. The most intricate patterns will unfold a world of beautiful balanced forms. With experience there will come the ability to compare work with work and composer with composer, penetrating many secrets of style, estimating merit and gladly recognizing mastery. The comparison of the music of a writer like Mendelssohn, who is often subject to rhythmic monotony, with the rhythmic affluence and constant surprise of Schubert or Schumann; the study of the remarkable development of Wagner in the command of this side of his art from "The Flying Dutchman" to "Tristan and Isolde"; the analysis of the subtleties and mannerisms of Brahms, of the resistless logic within the passionate ebb and flow of Beethoven, the solution of the rhythmic puzzles offered in some of the works of the Russian school — these interests enter strongly into the business of the music student; and as fast as they are brought to the attention of the amateur they enlarge the reach of his intelligent judgment. As the sounding shapes which once seemed all confusion begin to move in his consciousness in reasoned order and mutual aid his mind dilates with a sense of ease; he seems to play, as in a native element, in these waves of tone. The contrivances for temporary disturbance such as syncopation, irregular rhythm, and cross rhythm; interlacing curves in fugal counterpoint, where unlike melodic figures seem struggling for the mastery and rhythm seems lost in its own very abundance; the restraint of the tonal whirl from lawless confusion by the grasp of a few master figures or (as often in Beethoven) by a single master figure; the devices for imparting a sense of tension, concentration, and climax, or of relaxation, subsidence, and relief, — these tokens of creative genius, almost rivalling the living forms of nature in affluence and beauty, are to music what the nervous system is to the human organism. Through this vibrating network the soul of the music is revealed. It is not merely the means of obtaining unity amid diversity, it is the very life of music itself.

The close parallel that exists between the accents and rhythmic groupings of music and the posturings and evolutions of the dance is almost too obvious to require statement. It is not out of place, however, to call attention to the usefulness of dancing, both to the observer and the participant, through the exercise it affords to the rhythmic sense. The revival of the dance in our time on a higher plane than of old, both on the stage as an art of expression and in the public schools as a physical and æsthetic stimulus, is, I believe, a wholesome sign. The dance, like music, has a twofold æsthetic potency: first, of complex and unified movement, giving pleasure to the eye by its flowing lines that interweave in living patterns of grace, and second, the communication of mental states through the symbolism of posture and gesture. "The artistic dancer," says Mr. Bliss Carman, "uses bodily motion as a poet uses words, as a musician uses tones, as a painter uses colors—as an appeal not so much to our reason as to our sense and spirit—as a means of enlivening and gladdening our nature, making us more sensitive to beauty, more spontaneous in glad emotion, more sane and balanced in general well-being." That the art of dancing, once cultivated by philosophers, law givers, and priests as an essential in the training of the body and in the free play of the spirit, has been degraded in the uses of the modern stage, need not deceive us concerning its possibilities of beauty both physical and intellectual. We can have little conception of what the ancient dance was in the period of its ripest culture. A few passages in the old writings "send the imagination wistfully across the ages, straining, as it were, to see what must have been some of the loveliest scenes in Greek life" (Royal Cortissoz). The only adequate indication of what the dance must have been when treated with profound seriousness by a people to whom beauty was a constant necessity of life, is to be obtained from descriptions of Japanese dances, such as the account of the ceremonies of the Bon-odori, the Festival of the Dead, in Lafcadio Hearn's fascinating book, *Glimpses of Unfamiliar Japan.* A troop of girls are dancing in the moonlight in the temple court, near the ancient place of tombs:

"Under the wheeling moon, in the midst of the round, I feel as one within the circle of a charm. Verily this is enchantment; I am bewitched, bewitched by the ghostly weaving of hands, by the rhythmic gliding of feet, above all by the flitting of the marvelous sleeves—apparitional, soundless, velvety as a flitting of great tropical bats. . . . Always the white hands sinuously wave together as if weaving spells, alternately without and within the round, now with palms upward, now with palms downward; and all the elfish sleeves hover duskily together, with a shadowing as of wings; and all the feet poise together with such a rhythm of complex motion that, in watching it, one feels a sensation of hypnotism, as while striving to watch a flowing and shimmering of water. . . . More and more unreal the spectacle appears, with its silent smilings, with its silent bowings, as of obeisance to watchers invisible; and I find myself wondering whether, were I to utter but a whisper, all would not vanish forever, save the gray mouldering court and the desolate temple and the broken statue of Jizo, smiling always the same mysterious smile I see upon the face of the dancers."

Such enchantments can be woven by but two of the arts — the dance and music. What is music but the transmigration into tone of the immemorial and world-embracing spirit of the dance? In ancient times music was feeble and insignificant, but a compensation, almost an equivalent, was found in the beauty and expressiveness of bodily movement. The decline of the dance in modern times may be due to the development of a still nobler substitute. Not only the spirit, but the form of the dance has passed into modern music; historically the rhythms of instrumental music, and by adoption the rhythms of secular vocal music, are to a large extent derived from the popular dance. This may be almost intuitively discerned by one who, in listening to a performance by orchestra or piano, gives himself up, with closed eyes and rhythmic sense alert, to the swing and throb of the sounding forms. And whenever one has an opportunity to watch the dance in its best estate upon the stage, or in its most spontaneous form in folk dances, it will be found, I think, that the appreciation of the beauty that lies in music's "ideal motion" will be increased by the practice of the eye in tracing, amid the successions of bodily pose and gesture and evolution, the harmony of regulated and balanced change.

CHAPTER V

THE BEAUTY OF HARMONY

THE pleasure in melodic flow and rhythmic accent is universal except in the case of those unfortunates who are unable to recognize differences of pitch or regularity in recurring beats, and it requires, as I have tried to show, only such cultivation as will enable the hearer to follow composers in their elaboration of certain simple elements. With harmony, however, the case is somewhat different; a larger mental reach and a more tenacious grasp are required to comprehend its relations; and although individuals differ here as elsewhere, it may safely be said that a recognition of the beauty that lies in artistically managed combinations of simultaneous sounds and the richly varied color schemes of contrasted tonalities is the last among the musical appreciations to be acquired. Since the progressive development of harmony did not begin until as late as the twelfth century, it has been the fashion even among historians of music to ignore the existence of any harmonic sense up to that time, holding that the music of primitive and ancient peoples is unison only. This view can no longer be maintained, for it is certain that many savage tribes recognize the existence of musical intervals, that they often sing two and even more parts, and it is more than probable that similar experiments were made among the cultivated nations of antiquity. Professor John C. Fillmore, who made extensive researches in the music of the North American Indians, was undoubtedly not deceived in the apparent pleasure manifested by some of his dusky friends when their unison melodies were supplied with simple chords. What we call the beginning of counterpoint and harmony in the Middle Ages was merely the first fruitful recorded attempt to devise a system and evolve a theory of harmonic relations; the demand for a richer and more expressive utterance than successions of single tones could supply already lay dimly in the human consciousness. The dependence of melody upon harmony must also be recognized. Wallaschek justly remarks that "there is of course no doubt that our feeling for and comprehension of harmony have been developed by time, but so has our feeling for melody." "Primitive harmony is no doubt very rude, but primitive melody is precisely of the same kind." "If we compare a modern song with an air of savage races we find the latter very short, restricted to two or three tones and the same phrase constantly repeated, while our musical themes are worked out, built up, prolonged and varied so as to form a coherent, elaborate melody." It does not follow that the inability of the savage to invent a tune of more than one kind of melodic figure is due to his deficient sense of harmony; it is probably due rather to his incapacity for sustained thought and invention, for the early Gregorian chant system, long before the employment of part singing in the church, contained melodies of great length, elaborateness, and variety. But these Gregorian melodies are at the same time rambling and for the most part irregular, except so far as the text to which they are set gives them something like rhythmic order; it is only on the basis of definite tonality and the relationship of tonalities involved in chord structure that a melody that is proportioned, balanced, and satisfying to the modern ear can be developed.

This process was long ago virtually completed and the psychologic results of it have become the inheritance of every person that is in any way susceptible to the influences of music. The fact remains, however, that a consciousness of the beauty and the technical wonders of modern harmony is, with the average untrained music lover, the weakest of all the impressions that compose his musical world. It is true, of course, that the modern ear, however unrefined, takes cognizance of a chord as a concrete entity, so that the most unmusical person feels that something is lacking when a singer sings or a violinist plays without accompaniment. Nevertheless, with the common man the harmonic images are rather nebulous and countless beauties that enchant the musician are to him practically non-existent. His hearing of a musical performance, so far as harmony is concerned, is like indirect vision to a stroller out of doors. In the latter case there is a dull consciousness of a multitude of shapes and lights and colors forming a sort of misty fringe around the objects directly perceived; in the former a stream of sounds various in force, color, and fulness of texture, but unruled by any obvious plan, and with a thousand points of interest blurred in the mass.

The musical inquirer, therefore, will seek the advice that will aid him in developing the faculty by which he may select, compare, and comprehend while dealing with chord progressions and combinations of moving parts. The amateur whom I have in mind will be content with the outlines of the vast science of harmony—just enough to enable him to sift the masses of sound that enter his brain and to recognize in them a certain reason and order. He should be initiated into a few of the fundamental distinctions of consonance and dissonance, of major and minor, of diatonic and chromatic harmony, of cadence and half-cadence, of affiliations and oppositions among tonalities, of modulation, of the means by which logical relations and symmetrical design are accomplished in the succession of contrasted keys. The reason is clear—even a smattering of theoretical knowledge puts the hearer on the watch, and he is able to capture fugitive beauties that once eluded him. It can be shown by examples how sometimes a striking point in the melody really depends for its effect upon a peculiar harmonic change; how harmony is sometimes used merely to support and enrich the melody, again for the sensuous delight in sonorous and gorgeously colored chords, and again as a means of definite, characteristic expression. The learner must form the habit of listening down through the tone substance, following the movement of successive figures in the inner and lower parts, instead of confining his direct attention to the upper voice. He must be vigilant to catch the ceaseless changes of consonance and dissonance, of major and minor, of open and close harmony, and the most delicate contrasts of harmonic color. He may begin with the simpler harmonies, the so-called diatonic, in which key changes by sharps, flats, and naturals are few and slight; choosing German chorales, or themes for variation by Beethoven, or simple songs by the great German Lied writers, in order that he may learn to appreciate the beauty that lies in plain solid harmony as handled by masters. Comparing these with the thin popular ditties of the day he will at once obtain an insight that will be little short of a revelation. After that, his ear may be practiced in more richly colored and more intricate patterns, until the treasures of the great modern harmonists—the Wagners, the Chopins, the Griegs, the Francks—will charm without tantalizing him.

The difficulty of learning to follow harmonic

progressions is not so great as at first appears. For a chord, like a single tone, is one thing and not three or four things—that is, so far as the immediate impression is concerned. The musician, as Browning's Abt Vogler puts it, frames out of three sounds "not a fourth sound, but a star." These starry things called chords are almost infinite in their possibilities of color arrangement. When we count up the triads, sevenths, ninths, and altered chords in the major and minor keys the number is by no means immense, but their available combinations are practically endless. The finest ear will miss a great deal in rapid passages abounding in chromatic changes, and the wise music lover will take pains to hear copiously harmonized pieces over and over again. As in any exercise of the senses, improvement comes with practice; and when guided by a few general principles, and with the habit formed of listening to everything from the bottom to the top, he will finally obtain possession of an enjoyment which, it seems to me, is greater and more lasting than even the pleasure in melody and rhythm. It is a fact with most music lovers that melody and rhythm, captivating at first, will sooner or later lose their welcome freshness, while a fine bit of harmony gives a satisfaction that no amount of repetition can diminish.

The method of listening to all the simultaneous parts at once must also be employed in hearing songs, operas, solo performances of violin music—

everything in which a performer plays or sings a single part with the accompaniment of another instrument or an orchestra. The majority of listeners to fine singing or violin playing are hardly conscious of the accompaniment at all, although, as in an immense amount of the later dramatic and concert music, a large proportion of the beauty and expression, often the leading melody itself, is given to the orchestra or the piano. The modern song, for example, is very often a duet for voice and instrument, and the hearer who attends only to one part misses the half or more than half. Mr. Lawrence Gilman is quite right in saying that instead of finding fault with Wagner's works on the ground that the vocal parts are without musical interest or emotional meaning when detached from the orchestral support, one should see that the same thing is true of any writing for the voice allied with modern harmony in the accompaniment. Inexperienced music lovers are constantly falling into mistakes of judgment when they disparage vocal works because the voice part does not carry them away on tuneful wings. Let them give heed to the accompaniment and there they will find their recompense.

The ear must also be persuaded to the acceptance of combinations at which it naturally rebels. The experience of the race of musicians who in ancient Greece and the European Middle Ages knew only the octave, fifth, and fourth as consonances, afterward admitted thirds and sixths, but balked at sevenths unprepared; then snatched a fearful joy from haphazard sharps and flats; then long afterward proceeded from the diatonic principle to the chromatic, accepted the harshest dissonances, and now have become reconciled to the audacities of Strauss and Debussy and talk bravely of quarter steps in the good days to come, —this experience of the race often finds a reduced analogue in that of the music lover who trustfully allows his appreciation of novel effects of sound to grow by exercise. As he becomes familiar with the achievements of the masters in applying to expressive uses the endless resources of harmony, he is almost ready to declare, not that he is developing a latent faculty, but acquiring a new one. He hears what he never heard before, and with each new experience his powers of observation and coördination increase. He perceives that music has more dimensions than he had supposed. He learns to delight in the collision of masses with masses, of the infinite gradations of tone color as chord impinges against chord, dissonances resolve into consonances, the fair-hued threads of sound intertwine in patterns as subtle as those woven upon Oriental looms, no longer seeming incoherent and purposeless but obedient to an intelligent will which brings light and order out of chaos.

Then there is counterpoint, that austere and intricate science, the *bête noire* of students and amateurs. Entrance must be made into this labyrinth, just far enough to enable the ear to adjust itself to follow a number of simultaneous melodic parts, and obtain the definite impression that follows the recognition of organized plan. The learner would do well to add subject, answer, counter-subject, imitation, stretto, and episode to his interesting collection of technical specimens, but he need not be confused by a multitude of contrapuntal subtleties that do not contribute to the actual pleasure of his hearing. When he learns to divide his attention between two melodic progressions (a feat which Rousseau in a paradoxical moment pronounced impossible) he is on the borders of a new world; he will at last discover an unimagined pleasure in tracing the concurrent progress of three or four semi-independent parts as they wreathe themselves together in supple designs; he will wonder at the composer's skill, and the climaxes will produce a tenfold effect by reason of his ability to follow their cumulative preparation. It must not be forgotten that form in itself, however correct, is not necessarily a beautiful thing, as we speak of musical beauty. The tedious sonatas of Czerny and the immortal sonatas of Beethoven are built upon the same general scheme of design, and the cleverest and most regular fugue may be unutterably dreary. The recognition of contrapuntal structure is but a means to an end; the beauty of a fugue, like the beauty of any other musical work, is one of melody, harmony, and rhythm, and the listener should keep his mind open to these, relying upon his acquaintance with structural devices to adjust his perceptions at the proper focus.

In order that the student may appreciate the value of a fugue he must also be taught what *not* to expect, for if he looks for the buoyant sweeping melody, stirring dance rhythms, and pungent harmonic contrasts of the freer modern forms, his disappointment will blind him to the special characteristic beauties that actually lie before him. Beautiful bits of melody occur incessantly in the fugues of Bach, but they may be called incidental rather than primary, restricted by the necessity that compels the melodic details to contribute to the working out of a somewhat rigid scheme of design. In the nature of the case their purpose seems decorative rather than emotional. The fugue is more general in its expression than most other musical forms; it is not the natural channel for individual feeling. Hence the contrapuntal style has always been extensively employed in church music, for here the suggestion must be that of an abstract devotional mood, rather than the projection of an impassioned individual sentiment. As a means of training the ear, however, the fugue is of unequalled value in the appreciation of the new music as well as of the old. For, beginning with the later works of Beethoven, the polyphonic principle has been asserting itself more and more, under modified conditions, in every form of music. Following the modern tendency toward fulness and complexity and the enrichment of every detail, all the masters of the later time have plunged into the most exhaustive contrapuntal studies, and the works of Wagner, Brahms, Strauss, Debussy, Elgar, Franck are hardly less marvels of abstruse learning than those of the great contrapuntists of the eighteenth century. Witness the simultaneous presence of the three leading themes in the Overture to "The Mastersingers of Nuremberg" — indeed the whole score of this drama is a representative instance. Hardly less in the works of Schubert, Schumann, Chopin, Grieg, MacDowell — to mention only a few of the romantic group — must we learn to divide our consciousness and listen not merely for chord masses and surface melody, but also for the rise and fall of inner voices. In songs, piano pieces, religious music, operas, chamber music, symphonies, the polyphonic method plays so huge a rôle that without the ability to discover and trace the movement of simultaneous parts whole treasuries of expression will be locked in darkness, and the key that might open the casket lost beyond recovery.

In view of these facts there is no more useful practice for the music lover who is training his perceptions than listening to string quartet performances. Here are no sensational effects, no dazzling displays of tone color as in orchestral music, no overwhelming masses of sound, no vivid contrasts, nothing to bewilder, nothing to distract the attention from the melodic outlines; the physical materials are reduced almost to the lowest terms. Each instrument carries on a silver thread of melody; each has an equal right to consideration. Success in string quartet writing involves the ability to handle four melodic voices with the utmost skill of the contrapuntist's art. The pleasure that the mind of the hearer receives greatly consists in tracing the ingenious and graceful lines as they interweave into a tissue of intricate and constantly varied patterns. He must follow four voices at once, so that no grace of melody or delicacy of shading on the part of any instrument shall escape his notice. This affords a conclusive test by which the music lover may know how far the training of his ear has proceeded.

The practical conclusion to be drawn from the discussion of technique and form which has hitherto occupied us, is that the proper hearing of music demands the ability to hold the attention fixedly for considerable periods of time upon one order of impressions. No argument is required to show that the power of close unwavering attention is the prime condition of any worthy intellectual acquisition. Most people are defective in this power of sustained observation, and there is no more efficient corrective than a conscientious, determined study of musical works through the ear. It is undoubtedly more difficult to attend to a succession of auditory images than to visual images. This is true even in single impressions; whereas in music there are many simultaneous attacks upon the ear. Consider what it means to listen to an orchestral performance — to observe the concurrent threads of melody with the multitude of rhythmic figures, the resulting harmonies, modulations, and changes of tonality; to identify the different instruments and seize the ever-shifting gleams of tone color in their multifarious combinations. In the concert hall the eye must suspend its usual activities, the mind must cease that aimless wandering which is its usual occupation with all of us. Careful listening to music is an exercise in mental athletics, and the ability, which grows with discipline, to hold the volatile thought in the firm clutch of the will is not the least of the serious music student's gains.

CHAPTER VI

PERFORMANCE: THE ART OF THE PIANIST

Reference has already been made to the obvious fact that the impressions of music depend upon the abilities of an interpreter or a group of interpreters, added to those of the composer; that while an expert musician can derive considerable satisfaction from silent score reading, the ordinary music lover is in no such happy case, but must obtain his musical joys by the grace of certain people who perform in his presence for hire or good will. Moreover, the question of skill and imagination on the part of the performers enters so largely into the problem, that the very quality of beauty lies almost as much in their control as it does in the brain of the composer, so that to an inferior composition there may be imparted an unexpected charm, or a masterpiece be made almost ridiculous. Besides this, there are elements of delightfulness in performance which do not enter into the composer's calculation at all, but belong to the special technique of reproduction. The enjoyment of music, therefore, involves an appreciation of the art of the performer, and the music lover who is undergoing education in the practice of listening must acquire knowledge of the principles and methods of playing and singing in their various departments.

I have chosen to confine the discussion of these principles to the specific instances of piano playing and solo singing. A study of performance by orchestra, string quartet, and chorus, and upon violin, organ, and other instruments would involve a great deal of repetition, and does not seem to me to be required in view of the discursive purpose of this volume. The lover of music should certainly become familiar with the constitution of the orchestra, the powers and limitations of the violin and organ, and the general laws that distinguish choral song from solo singing and orchestral playing. Instruction in these matters can easily be obtained by inquiries from experts, or from certain excellent treatises which this book of mine is not required to duplicate. I have selected piano playing and solo singing because they come constantly into the music lover's experience, and because they are typical of performance in general. The principles of musical expression are very much the same whatever the medium employed, and the amateur who is able to judge intelligently the work of a pianist or vocalist will only require acquaintance with a few technical matters to receive right impressions from all the other means of interpretation.

Let me pass at once, then, to the question of performance in general and afterward to the discussion of the particular departments of the performer's art which I have chosen.

There are so many applications of the word art to activities that are diverse, from the "art" of swimming or fencing, to poetry or sculpture, that in our despair of finding a common basis for them all we sometimes resolve to refuse the designation to any but a very restricted and unquestionable category. When a distinct and permanent "work of art" is produced, one shaped out of preëxisting materials, designed for self-expression or the giving of pleasure rather than for utilitarian or didactic ends, or where a decorative value is added to practical convenience—in such products of design and fancy as a memorial arch, a poem, a statue, a picture, a piece of music, a chiselled vase, or jewelled ornament—we are on safe ground when we speak of the laws and methods of fine art.

There appears now another division of activities to which in common parlance the name of art is applied, in which an impression of ordered and imaginative beauty is conveyed, but without any embodiment of the impulse in tangible or enduring shape. I refer to the arts of performance, such as dancing, acting, poetic recitation, and musical reproduction. In what sense are these functions artistic? Is the term by which they are honored in common speech justified to the reason?

It is evident that there is need here of still another classification. Dancing stands apart from the other activities mentioned in that no "work of art" is at hand, no score, text, or design to which one may refer for suggestion or comparison; the means of effect are bodily movements and attitudes which vanish with the moments in which they appear. They had, indeed, a previous ideal existence in the mind of the performer, and they have a subsequent existence in the memory of the spectator, but there is nothing to which the term *form* can be applied, and so far from there being anything concrete or tangible involved the display is a vision which comes from the void and into the void returns. Nevertheless it would seem pedantic utterly to refuse the term art to dancing in its best estate. It is not merely the overflow of physical health and vigor in moving lines of grace—it is not wholly sensuous, but is capable of a wide range of emotional expression. Among the Greeks and the Japanese—nations preëminently endowed with the love of beauty in form and movement—the dance was and is esteemed an art worthy of the supervision of the best minds—an art pleasing to men and gods. And although in modern times, at least as a stage entertainment, it has fallen from its former dignity, there are signs that a revival is at hand, and the dance, refined and regulated, may take a higher place than it has lately held among the agencies that quicken the sense of beauty and promote health of body and mind.

Still less are we justified in refusing the title of art to the actor's craft. In certain particulars his work is related to that of the dancer, in that he employs means that are not external to himself but are identified with his own physical organization. In the use of different timbres and degrees of vocal force for purposes of expression he is allied to the singer. In his case also there is produced no "work of art" which survives the moment of presentation. The actor stands apart from the dancer and undoubtedly above him, in that the actor's whole aim is to present in visible and audible guise conceptions of the mind which have already been put into permanent literary form. This work of literary art, however, is not yet complete; an essential element is lacking. A play is not a literary work merely; the actor adds an element which fulfils the intention of the author, and in so doing he shows himself not a mechanical imitator but a collaborator who contributes something individual and original. Many effective plays could be named in which, during entire scenes, the poetic idea is largely conveyed by vocal timbre, facial expression, attitude, gesture, and the various details known as "business," the words alone seeming to offer nothing very significant. Indeed, complete plays, such as the famous *L'Enfant prodigue*, have been performed in dumb show, plays abounding in incident, with interesting development of plot and character. Let one read the text of the scene in which Macbeth, with his mind keyed to its murderous intent, has the hallucination of a dagger in the air. One may read the lines and not be greatly moved; but let one witness the scene as realized in the actual presentment by a competent actor, and it will appear that the poet's words are hardly more than a suggestion from which the player creates a terrible picture of a man in whose soul ambition, fear, compassion, and incipient remorse are fiercely contending. A painter might portray Macbeth at this moment and his picture would be a work of art; the actor's performance is likewise the outcome of thought, design, adaptation of means to an end first conceived in the imagination, lacking only the element of permanence in some form that can be touched and reproduced in a copy. None the less is it art, for the poet's words are but symbols and indications; they are tame and cold until the actor, employing vocal sounds and bodily organs as material, brings the thought in its fulness to the eye and ear of the beholder.

The arts of poetry, painting, and sculpture, therefore, reproduce phenomena of nature and human emotion with something added, viz., the personality of the artist. The actor's craft is an art by second intention, in which literary expression, already reproduction, passes through a second process, and becomes subject to another addition. Each process is art, because something preëxisting in more or less crude and unorganized form is worked over by a new application of emotion and contrivance into a beautiful embodiment of an idea.

Now music as an art is nearly allied to the drama in that the work of the original creator remains in abeyance, in an embryo state we might say, awaiting the second birth through which it enters into completeness of life. This subsequent activity under the hands of the performer is likewise a result of artistic contrivance; we call it reproductive, but like the actor's portrayal it is much more than that. The performer is not concerned simply with transmitting the intention of the composer—the composition is a medium by which he confides to his hearers an emotion that has become his own. It is well enough to say as a counsel of moderation that the player or singer should lay aside self-consciousness and love of personal display and devote himself to the interpretation of the composer's thought, but in fact, since he is himself endowed with a musical temperament, with the craving for self-expression that belongs to every normal human being, he cannot efface himself and become literally and completely the author's tool. His very constitution that turns him to the study and practice of music implies a certain likeness between his impulse and that of the composer. The black symbols upon the page are transmuted into living voices. The performer forgets that they have been loaned to him to use as the composer's representative, he conceives them as his own; they are his own for the moment, and if he be truly a master he persuades the hearer into the same belief.

In this process the performer, of course, expresses himself not as he is in the constant relations of daily life, but as he is in the mood of exaltation excited by the touch of the music. His effort, like that of the actor, is the deliberately imaginative one of identifying himself with the work in hand. There is a sort of double consciousness at work. Without the loss of self-control and the power of instant adaptation of means to ends, he sinks himself in the substance of the composition and lives its life, which for the time being is the whole of life for him. This is the explanation of the power of great performers upon the stage or the concert platform. The player feels no difference between the rôle or the music and his own personality. What was external has become internal. There is a large margin of self-determination allowed him; the author's conception is given to him temporarily for his personal use, and he making it his own remoulds it nearer to his heart's desire.

No other art, not even the drama, is so dependent upon a mediator as music. Music unperformed is a dead thing, and there is no medium into which it can be translated. On the musical staff the notes are stationary; they imply motion but they do not move. The rapidity of the succession of sounds, their grouping and shading, are determined to a large extent by the player's thought. The composer, to be sure, gives all the general directions in regard to tempo, dynamics, etc., and there are certain principles and traditions which are generally accepted and handed down by authority; but in art, laws are very frequently repealed, and precedents have no power of self-enforcement. In spite of all checks and balances the composer is quite at the performer's mercy. Wagner attributed the failure of the "Tannhäuser" overture at its first performance at Leipzig to the lack of understanding of the work on the part of the conductor. Franz Liszt, in one of his *Travel Letters of a Bachelor of Music*, complains bitterly of the misunderstanding on the part of the audience from which composers often suffer by reason of unintelligent performance. "The poet, the painter, or the sculptor," he says, "brings his work to completion in the quiet of his atelier, and when it is completed, there are publishers to circulate it, or museums in which it may be exhibited; no mediation is necessary between the art work and its judges. The composer, on the other hand, must have recourse to interpreters who are often incompetent or indifferent, and make him suffer by reason of a rendering that is perhaps true to the letter, but utterly fails to reveal the thought of the work and the genius of the author."

We have all heard pianists who were easily masters of every mechanical difficulty, but whose playing was cold and monotonous. Nothing is more common in musical criticism than the complaint that a certain pianist has failed to grasp the essential mood of a musical work or the spirit of a composer. This player, it may be said, is a master of technique, but he should not try to play Chopin. Another is at home in the late romantic school, but he has no proper conception of Bach or Beethoven. Another turns a bold and passionate fancy of Schumann into a bit of sentimental trifling. Another, inferior to many in brilliancy, illùminates everything he plays, and imparts to long familiar compositions an unsuspected eloquence. As the works of the great composers pass through the hands of skilled and sympathetic performers they are constantly revealing new beauties. A pianist who is on the road to mastership, and even after he has attained that exalted degree, keeps certain great works constantly before him, and as the years go on his playing of them is more or less insensibly modified, changing with his mental growth, with his experience of life and art. Alexander McArthur tells us that a pupil once protested to Rubinstein that since he knew the "Waldstein" sonata thoroughly he did not need to practise it any longer. "Don't you?" said Rubinstein sadly; "Well, you are eighteen and I am sixty. I have been half a century practicing that sonata and I need still to practice it. I congratulate you." No thought here on the part of the great Russian that a musical piece is a finality whose reproduction requires only technical dexterity and obedience to rules. I can even conceive it possible that a musical work may take a deeper place in the soul of a student than it had in the mind of its author. Handel would probably be much astonished if he knew the uses to which his "Largo" (originally a song to a plane tree in his opera

"Xerxes") has been put. One who has felt his whole being quiver under Mischa Elman's marvelous performance of Schubert's "Ave Maria" may easily believe that the composer's intention was more than fulfilled. Anton Seidl, it is said, could not conduct the last movement of Tchaikovsky's "Symphonie pathétique" without tears. Was Seidl simply following the directions of the score, and was the result only a matter of formal prescription and drill? When the orchestra, submissive to his will, extorted the very last throb of anguish from those amazing chords, had Seidl no share in the creative act? If one denies that he had, perhaps it would be convincing to hear the work (as was once my misfortune) performed by an orchestra as competent as Seidl's, but led by a conductor inferior to him not only in musicianship, but also in imagination and sensitiveness of heart.

It has become a frequent complaint among the musical critics of the press that pianists as a rule refuse to present new works to the public, confining their programs to a limited range of standard compositions of masters who are dead. There is good ground for this dissatisfaction on the part of those who have the progressive interests of art in view. It is probable, however, that the generality of listeners are contented with this condition and there are certain obvious reasons why they are so. There is one possible explanation that is not quite so obvious, and that is that every famous work is in one sense a novelty when performed by a great pianist. "Hamlet" and "Romeo and Juliet," supremely great as they are as literary works, would hardly maintain their attracting power generation after generation if their leading rôles were always acted in precisely the same manner in every detail. It is not simply "Hamlet" or "Romeo and Juliet" that one goes to see, but Forbes-Robertson's Hamlet, it may be, or Julia Marlowe's Juliet. And so when a veteran concert goer pays his fee to hear a famous pianist play the "Sonata Appassionata" or Schumann's Concerto, it is not merely to hear an old work, every note of which he can anticipate, but a work renewed under the individual treatment of the player. From Harold Bauer he will receive one impression, from Pachmann another, from Careño another, from Mrs. Zeisler or Hofmann or Godowski a "reading" that is different still. No performance of a classic is ever final. There is always something to be said by the next comer. There are two factors in the exhibition, and the second can never be calculated. The charm of musical performance is partly the charm of surprise. Zola defined a work of art as a bit of nature seen through a temperament. In music, as in a drama, there is a second intermediary stage, and in playing, singing, or conducting we have a work of art seen through a temperament. The performer receives the work from the author, and when he gives it forth again it has undergone a mysterious change. It has not simply been touched with new color, it has been quickened with a new spirit.

In all this there may be found, I think, the reply to those who protest against the "star system." They are right, of course, when admiration of the star means indifference to the composition, or if that admiration is directed solely to mere tricks of virtuosity. But they are wrong if they overlook the fact that the star is or may be also an artist who creates the work anew at every representation; that in music the work and the performance cannot be separated in consciousness; that the greater the performance the greater the work.

The lover of music finds, therefore, that he must know something of the laws of performance as well as the laws of composition. What is good playing and good singing? he will ask. In what is one executant superior to another? Are there rules by which judgment can be guided? An intelligent person does not wish to applaud a defective performance any more than he is content to enjoy a poor composition. He wants not only an opinion of his own, but also reasons with which to confirm it. The hopeless differences of view among his critical friends over the merits of this or that performer may perhaps give him pause by showing him that infallibility is not attainable. This is true, however, in all art matters; it does not follow that there are no principles by which one may be guided to safe and sane conclusions.

The music lover whom I have in mind in all these discussions is called, not so much to bestow awards of praise or censure, as to observe, appreciate, and enjoy. The appraisal of values, leading to judgments, will follow enlightenment, but inquiry must come first. The question, therefore, is similar to that which we have already considered in our study of form and composition—what does musical performance offer us? What are we to look for in playing or singing? And also—following the line which we have opened in the beginning of this chapter—what does the performer add out of his own taste, knowledge, and genius? What does he do that is not commanded him by the composer? Then, finally, what is the distinction between good and evil in musical reproduction?

Taking piano playing as a type of musical performance in general, for reasons already given, we have now to ask—in what respect is the pianist an artist? What is his part in determining the character of a composition as it reaches the listener's ear? He has before him a number of leaves of paper on which are printed certain black characters, most of them notes and rests, others consisting of indications for delivery. A very slight consideration shows that the notes and other conventional signs which compose a musical score direct the player's action up to a certain point and there leave him. There are slight variations of tone length, regulations of speed from moment to moment, contrasts and blendings of shades, refined use of the pedals, subtleties of phrasing—in a word, a host of sensitive adjustments which constitute expression and impart life, buoyancy, and finesse. These cannot be indicated with precision by the system of notation as it now exists. Fortunate indeed are we that it is so, for were it otherwise the player's task would afford but little inspiration; two pianists of equal technical skill would produce exactly the same effect. The inexhaustible charm of the masterworks, however, lies largely in the fact that no such mechanical reiteration is possible. The most stolid piano thumper that ever tormented a critical audience must give something that has not precisely existed before. His performance, as Touchstone said of Audrey, may be a poor thing but it is his own. On the other hand if the pianist is a man of genius we have the splendid spectacle of two original forces at work. Liszt's playing of Beethoven, writes Wagner, "was not mere reproduction, but real production." There is fire in every great work, but it is latent and must be rekindled under the breath of the player's will.

It may be necessary to remind the reader at this point (and I ask him to bear it in mind all through this discussion) that the determination of the player in regard to the "reading" of musical works is very plainly, one may say narrowly, restricted. His freedom is not license. No capricious or spasmodic renderings are to be tolerated. Maupassant's injunction to the novelist—"give us something fine according to your temperament"—may be applied to the pianist, but he must remember that it will not be fine unless it conforms to the eternal laws of art. He must look up to the composer as his master. His work must be chastened by reverence. He must not wilfully push his own personality into the foreground, and by a false straining after originality, by mannerisms and exaggerations, do violence to the author's intentions. He has many guides in history, scholarship, and tradition that must be respected. This side of the vexed question of the pianist's duty will be considered later; meanwhile a recognition of it must be held in reserve while we go on to consider the privileges of the player as an original thinker.

In a letter discussing certain points in piano playing Edward MacDowell once wrote, "Black notes on white paper are the despair of composers." He meant by this that our system of notation is incomplete, so that while the composer can show what notes are to be sounded, he is only partly able to indicate in what manner they are to be sounded, and consequently is more or less at the mercy of the performer. I have tried to prove that the art gains more than it loses by this state of things, and that the world of performers and music lovers will never share the composer's regret. Let us now come close to details, and taking the words of MacDowell as a text inquire just what are the elements of performance that cannot be set down in black notes on white paper.

Take first the question of tempo. The composer puts at the head of his piece a direction, consisting of a word or two, which shows his wish as to the general rate of speed, such as Adagio,

Andante, Allegro. No one supposes that these or other expressions of the same nature signify an exact number of beats to the minute. Adagio means slowly or leisurely, but the Italian word is as indefinite as the English. Andante may indicate one pace to one person, another to another, and to the same person it will vary with the composition. Wagner explains that there are two kinds of Allegro movement, each requiring a special kind of treatment. Sebastian Bach did not put directions for tempo at the head of his pieces; who shall determine at what rate of speed they should be played? Metronome marks are more exact, but they are far from being an infallible reliance. At the most they indicate the general movement of a composition, not the alterations that must constantly occur. They often serve as fetters to players or conductors that submit to them. Wagner at one time made extensive use of them in his dramas, but afterward decided that it was best on the whole to leave the question of tempo to the taste and musicianship of the conductor.

The amount of time to be occupied in the performance of a composition as a whole is, however, the easiest part of the problem. Rarely does a piece of considerable length or variety of style require an exactly uniform rate of motion from beginning to end. The beauty of an interpretation consists to a very large extent in the varying degrees of speed in the different divisions, periods, and phrases. It is the feature to which the composer gives the least thought in his orders to the player, and consequently it is in this particular that pianists are most at variance with one another. Nowhere else are taste and judgment more in demand than here; nowhere else are perversions and eccentricities more abundant. Condemnations by critics of the "conceptions" of players or conductors will be found in the great majority of cases to apply to tempo. Wagner goes so far as to say that "the whole duty of a conductor is comprised in his ability always to indicate the right tempo. His choice of tempi will show whether he understands the piece or not. With good players the true tempo induces correct phrasing and expression." The determination of the "true tempo," however, is not so easy. "I have often been astonished," says Wagner again, "at the singularly slight sense for tempo and execution evinced by leading musicians." In spite of uncertainty in the practical application of the principle of speed variation, in the privilege itself is found the element which gives to music its delightful suggestion of ease, grace, and elasticity. A too rigid tempo gives a suggestion of friction, of resistance somewhere; a flexible tempo is motion as free, confident, and joyous as the flowing of winds or ocean tides. Those buoyant fluctuations of movement that we hear in a masterly performance, those unexpected contrasts, those languishing retards, those fiery accelerations, those delicate balancings of phrase against phrase, those affectionate lingerings upon lovely modulations, those almost imperceptible delays as if to give a beautiful chord a little more time to resound along the corridors of the memory, those tender caressing familiarities, those impetuous defiances, all those bold liberties which prove the tone masses submissive to the player's will, the direct manifestation of his emotion—how eloquent, how illuminating they are!

That the composer should say to the player that here and here, and thus and thus, shall he make these expressive alterations of speed is impossible. Rarely does he attempt to do so. Here and there he will write ritardando or accelerando, but precisely how much slower or faster, or exactly at what instant these changes begin, cannot be indicated. In the wide spaces of the piece, however, no directions are given. The composer implicitly says to the player: In the matter of tempo I put myself in your hands, your musicianship is the arbiter; if my music sounds dull and monotonous you must take a part or the whole of the blame, if otherwise a goodly share of the honor shall be yours.

It is well known that it is Chopin who has brought the beauty that lies in tempo modification most palpably into notice, and that under the title tempo rubato, or "stolen time," it has become, we might say, self-conscious. These liberties, however, are not as lawless as the term would seem to imply, for the alterations of tempo that give elasticity to a performance are so adjusted and balanced in good playing that the sense of poise is never lost. Like all other elements of expression they must be regulated by conscious artistic purpose. The very nature of Chopin's music implies this freedom of movement, but it is now granted, although in less degree, in the works of the classic masters. Even in Bach's fugues, where a machine-like stiffness once passed for orthodoxy, a more natural and human treatment is allowed. That this liberty may be abused we all know. There are agreements among musicians that have acquired the binding force of laws, and must not be violated at the player's caprice. A prelude by Bach or an adagio by Beethoven is of a more rigid mould than a nocturne by Chopin and must be rendered with more sobriety and reserve. The player must constantly remind himself that freedom in tempo does not mean unsteadiness, and that the rate of speed in each phrase does not depend solely upon its own separate interest, but still more upon its relation to its companion phrases. We must have in music a sense of equilibrium, of stability. A careless, spasmodic hurrying and retarding leads only to flabbiness and inconsequence.

The second of the constituents of expression that rest mainly upon the player's determination consists in differences of loudness and softness, also known as nuance, or light and shade. The composer makes a rather liberal use of the marks for different degrees of force, such as f., p., sf., cres., dim., but every pianist knows that it is for himself to decide just how these signs shall be interpreted, and also that his performance must be full of accents and modifications of tone volume which the writer does not attempt to indicate. Composers differ greatly in the abundance of their dynamic signs, but at the best they can do no more than suggest the relative values of these changes, while the absolute values, the exact amount of force, depend upon the player's physical command of tone, the construction of his instrument, and still more upon his musical feeling and judgment. Even the extreme marks pp. (softest) and ff. (loudest) are indefinite. The softest possible and the loudest possible are never indulged in by a player of discretion. Not only must fortissimo be subjected to the final law of tone beauty (in spite of the fact that this law is often grossly violated by famous pianists) but its degrees vary greatly according to circumstances. A rapid run in single notes cannot possibly be made as loud as a detached chord, although the composer may use the ff. sign for both. On the other hand, the softest possible tone would be inaudible except perhaps to the performer himself. If these extreme signs are so inexact, what shall be said of the grades between, only a few of which are designated by the composer? The printed dynamic signs are like the more obvious elevations and depressions in a distant landscape—innumerable are the undulations between.

Even the signs which the composer takes pains to insert are often ignored by the player, sometimes justly, sometimes unjustly. I have heard

Anton Rubinstein make a diminuendo in a Beethoven sonata where the author had written a crescendo, and vice versa. What pianist ever ends Chopin's delicate F sharp Impromptu with a crash, as the composer seems to demand? Mr. W. S. B. Mathews tells that he once prepared a class for MacDowell's "March Wind," which the composer was to play in public, that he carefully called attention to every nuance in the piece, and that to his consternation MacDowell played it fortissimo from beginning to end. The composer, certainly, has a larger privilege in respect to his own work than the ordinary performer, but this instance shows that he does not always attach the same seriousness to the expression marks that he does to the notes, and that within certain limits they may be considered as suggestive and provisional rather than arbitrary.

After all, it is the broader, more general scheme of light and shade that is furnished by the composer. The finer gradations, those subtle and immeasurable modifications of dynamic value which make a composition a palpitating, coruscating thing of beauty, are wholly under the player's will. The simplest piece is inexhaustible in the opportunities it affords for tone variety. Listen to a rapid, clearly articulated scale, filled with undulating crescendos and diminuendos and rhythmic accents. Listen to a surging double arpeggio, its waves of tone rising and falling as majestically as the billows of the sea. Or a series of pure sonorous chords, pressed with a perfect adaptation of the fingers in order to secure solidity and balance, with a melody singing brightly upon their surface. Or a skein of delicate filaments of sound, with a single rich tone ringing through them like the far-away call of a horn. These things are among the luxuries of sensation, and unlike many luxuries they bring no surfeit.

The study of these effects is for the pianist the task of a lifetime. The desire for tone beauty must be a veritable passion if he is ever to attain true artistry. Not less must the music lover appreciate its worth, ever be quick to detect it, and train his perceptions to respond to the most delicate gradations in beautiful sound both in nature and in art.

"The tone sustained with equal power," said Wagner, "is the basis of all expression." This was said of vocal and orchestral music, and although an evenly sustained tone is impossible with the piano (since by reason of the mechanism the tone diminishes from the instant it is struck) yet it has always hovered before the minds of the great players as an ideal, the very longing for it affecting their touch and treatment. To prolong the short and relatively dry tone of the piano to the greatest possible extent has always been the aim of manufacturers; but the limit is soon reached, and players are often forced to fall back upon a system of disguises and pretences, the instrument assuming a virtue that it does not possess. In gaining the notion of sustained tone without the actuality the listener's fancy works as well as that of the player. He is more credulous than any speculator. He wishes to be deceived. There are even ways by which a tone may apparently be made to swell after being struck—an effect that is very beautiful, and legitimate because beautiful.

We speak of a pianist's "singing touch" as one of his most admirable merits. There is no more frequent injunction at the present day than that the tone must have a pure singing quality, no matter how rapid, intricate, or violent the passage may be. "Do not think of striking your notes," exclaimed Rubinstein, "think of singing them!" This injunction forbids the short, dry, unsympathetic tone one often hears, as well as the harsh, brassy, clanging stroke in which even reputable players often indulge. In piano playing as well as in orchestral and violin playing the pure, rich, sustained tone of the human voice at its best must be the standard.

This problem involves also that of quality or timbre in piano tone, in respect to which there are many delusions abroad. It would be easy to show that the player has but very slight power—perhaps none at all—of altering the *quality* of tone by his way of pressing the keys, that force and duration are the only elements he can control by his touch alone, leaving out the modification that can be effected by the pedals. Nevertheless there is a vast difference in sheer sensuous tone beauty in the playing of different pianists. This is not the place to explain all the causes of these differences. They consist mainly, perhaps wholly, in extremely minute shades and degrees of blending and contrasting the two elements of duration and loudness. The love of color and the thought of color will, however, strongly influence the touch in piano music. Hans von Bülow sometimes suggested to his pupils that they think here and there of a flute, a 'cello or a horn. No one knew better than he that a pianist cannot in the least imitate the timbre of any orchestral instrument; piano tone is piano tone and never anything else. But the thought of an instrument so luscious in quality and so full in sustaining power as a 'cello or a horn would insensibly affect the touch and the disposal of dynamic relations. This modern emphasis upon tone color in piano playing is one manifestation of the universal demand for sensuous beauty in all art which is so marked a feature of our time. Color in painting, color in photography, color in orchestration, color in singing, color in piano playing — these are the response to the quickened sensitiveness of eye and ear which every new chromatic invention in picture or music helps in turn to promote. Artists even speak of color in an etching or engraving, meaning of course that color is suggested. And so in piano playing tone color is suggested, the mind is stimulated so that it impulsively throws over the music a sort of prismatic veil which is none the less delightful for being so largely an illusion. Art is full of suggestion, and it asks the beholder to coöperate with the producer. The whitest pigment is a thousand degrees less bright than sunlight, but De Hoogh and Turner and Monet paint sunlight to the perfect satisfaction of the observer. It is one of the wonders of music that an instrument essentially so cold and monochromatic as the piano can take on so many lovely tints and reënforce melody and harmony with sounds so delicious to the sensual ear. Of all this the composer, with his black notes on white paper, gives but a remote intimation. It is the contribution of the performer in his capacity of artist.

Another means of obtaining beautiful changes of tone color, to which the listener should attend, is in the use of the pedals. A master is known by his pedalling as well as by the exploits of his fingers. The composer or editor may, of course, set down pedal marks, but they are at the best inadequate, often inexact, and an experienced player gives little or no heed to them. Even to an immature performer they are an awkward kind of assistance and the sooner he learns to do without them the better. An accomplished pianist simply conceives a certain tone effect and employs the pedal for the production of that effect. He subjects tone adjustment by means of the pedals to an elaborate analysis, until at last, with the growth of experience, his pedalling becomes a second nature, and his foot responds to his thought as automatically as his hand.

The question now arises, What is it that the pedals do? There is probably no other feature in piano playing that is so misunderstood, not only by the general public but also by piano students. The pedal that is managed by the right foot is persistently called the "loud pedal," which designation is a complete misnomer. It is easy to see, if one thinks about it, that the damper pedal cannot possibly make the sounds louder. The degree of loudness in the case of a sounding string depends upon the amplitude of the vibrations, and in piano music the amplitude of the vibrations depends upon the amount of force with which the hammer comes against the string. When a single key is struck and the pedal is not pressed, a damper rises; when the pedal is pressed, all the dampers in the instrument are raised. This cannot affect the amplitude of the vibrations. Every player knows that the damper pedal enables him to continue the tone after his finger has left the key, — the most important mechanical invention in the history of the art, for without it our magnificent treasure of piano music, founded by Beethoven, could never have come into existence.

But the damper pedal, as I have already intimated, does more than sustain the tones that are struck; it makes them more rich and sympathetic to the ear and enables the player to obtain variety of tone color. It is easy to see how this is done. Every musical tone is compound instead of simple. A fundamental tone, indicated by a note upon the staff and produced by the vibration of the whole string, contains also other tones made by vibrations of parts of the string. These "resultant tones," "overtones," "harmonics," or "upper partials," as they are variously called, cannot ordinarily be distinguished from the fundamental tone, but they color it, imparting its peculiar quality or timbre. In a violin or clarinet these overtones are very prominent; in a flute or organ diapason pipe they are much less so. In the piano they are to be reckoned with. Put the damper pedal down and all the dampers are raised. That leaves all the strings free or "open," and some that are not struck will vibrate slightly by reason of the impingement upon them of the secondary air waves that are stirred by the string that is struck by the hammer. The strings whose vibration thus produced can be heard by the normal ear are those of the octave, the twelfth, and the second octave above the smitten string, and in a fine grand piano perhaps one or two more. It follows that the sounds that come from a piano are richer in quality when the damper pedal is used than when it is idle.

The soft pedal, which has but recently, comparatively speaking, come into its own as a means of tone beauty, does not merely make the sounds softer, it alters their timbre. In a grand piano it makes the hammer strike two strings instead of three; that alone would produce a modification of the tone, while at the same time the third string, although not touched, vibrates sympathetically with a delicate, veiled, shimmering quality that gives a peculiar mellow and sympathetic effect to the combined impression. The soft pedal takes from the instrument its characteristic brilliancy, affording such contrasts that the player will often employ it even with a strong touch, carrying the special effect produced by this apparatus into broad sonorous tone masses.

The study of the pianist in the use of the damper pedal, in spite of its coloristic possibilities, lies chiefly in its function as a tone-sustaining contrivance. The piano is unique among instruments in its ability to prolong tones when the player's fingers are busy with new ones, and the opportunities thus afforded for variety, fulness, and grandeur of tone effect are numberless. To press and release the pedal at exactly the proper instant, to produce continuity of sound with never the slightest confusion in the harmonies, to blend, distribute, and contrast all the varieties of tone color that are latent in the instrument without excess or barrenness, and to do all this without losing distinctness of articulation or blurring the outline of the rhythmic figure — here is a field of endless study for the player and delight to the appreciative listener. A pianist is indeed a past master of the art of pedalling when the most greedy ear is satisfied and the most sensitive ear can detect no flaw.

Last to be considered among the contributions made by the player is phrasing. This term signifies the disclosure to the ear of the rhythmic structure of a piece. The firm metrical basis and the intricate rhythmic figuration must be as distinctly in the consciousness of the player as in that of the composer. All the rhythmic laws of musical art must be familiar to him in practice if not in theory, and his skill of hand must so reënforce his sense of structural design that the listener will never be for a moment in doubt concerning the essential factors in the tonal ebb and flow. Under the player's hand the entanglements of the interwoven threads are unravelled. All becomes clear, symmetrical, orderly. He imparts to the music a suggestion of naturalness, of spontaneity; there is poise, buoyancy, and balance; there is the ecstasy of vibration, the throb of life. This art requires incessant study and the most vigilant care. There have been pianists, such as Hans von Bülow, who were especially distinguished for their clear-cut scholarly phrasing, other elements of effect being often sacrificed to that. Other players, who have delighted more in masses of sound and splendid tonal contrasts, have not taken such extreme pains to make every thread of tissue evident. We seem to have here two classes of pianists — the scholarly, reflective, and analytical, with an extremely refined sense of form; and the bold, impetuous, and impressionistic, whose minds are intent upon the broader lights and shades and masses rather than upon minute dissection. The first love to make the work transparent, holding to the light every detail of organization. The second will often obscure detail for the sake of breadth, concentration, and color. Either tendency in excess leaves something to be desired; the consummate artist of the keyboard will grant to every means of beauty its true measure, not sacrificing the mass for the sake of the parts nor the parts for the sake of the mass. He will finish each item cleanly, but will remember that motives and phrases, like the lines and colors of a painting, find their value not in isolation and detachment, but in their relation to one another and to the whole.

There are four means by which the structural grouping of tones is made apparent, viz. accents, alternations of longer and shorter tones, breaks in the succession of sounds (including phrasing by the damper pedal), and crescendo and diminuendo. In the application of these rhythmic devices the player is certainly more restricted than in the modification of tempo or in shading. It is a matter of knowledge with him, of musical scholarship, rather than of personal preference. That is to say, tempo and shading are very greatly subject to the player's feeling and imagination, and may measurably differ in the performance of the same composition by the same player at different times, or under the hands of players who are unlike one another in temperament. Phrasing, however, is either right or wrong; within the successions of melodies and harmonies there dwells the essential rhythmic design dictated by the inherent laws of musical construction. There is the metrical foundation established by the beat and the measure grouping, while the rhythmic figuration springs from it in tropical luxuriance. Both alike must be rescued from confusion and when offered to the ear brought under the control of artistic design. In effecting this the player must chiefly rely upon his scholarship and his musical instinct, for the means which the composer possesses for indicating the proper phrasing are very incomplete. This fact is made evident by the numerous and bewildering books on rhythm and the phrased editions of the classic composers — the product of an outlay of labor and thought of which the layman has little conception. An extensive knowledge of rhythmic laws and of the peculiar rhythmic styles of the great piano composers must be a part of the mental equipment of the pianist. In the digital analysis of the intricate minutiæ of structure the performer must give a multitude of accents not indicated in the general metrical scheme — he must often vary the time values of individual notes, must make breaks in the tone current which are not marked in the score, must use crescendo and diminuendo for the stirring of the rhythmic waves to their progressive rise and fall. The curving lines, or slurs, which abound in musical scores are sometimes employed as phrasing signs by composers, but so irregularly and with such disregard of system that the player who should direct his phrasing by them would produce the most unhappy results. Even the elucidations of scholarly editors do not always agree. It is only by a highly developed rhythmic sense, a firm grasp of musical structure, years of study and experience, a technique so perfect that in the most rapid and difficult passages every shade of tone and every variety of touch are under complete control, that a performer is able to solve all the mysteries of the phrasing art and become infallibly true to those laws of form that give to musical works their complex order, their inner logic, their plastic grace, and their architectonic strength.

The player who makes an intelligent study of rhythm will not confine his analysis to the smaller groupings of period and section and phrase, but will also attend to the larger divisions in which these are contained; he will hold in his mind the entire framework of the piece and will give to his hearers an impression of solidity and mutual support among the parts. In this, the highest grade of rhythmic interpretation, there will be heard marked dissimilarities among players. One will unravel the texture with the utmost care, separating the phrases and rounding off the outlines of all the details with an almost finical nicety, at the same time so regardless of the larger unity that the work will appear like a mosaic of brilliant spots with no suggestion of continuous development and comprehensive organization. I have heard the first movement of Beethoven's "Sonata Appassionata" so treated — each phrase highly polished but no grasp of the movement in its vast reach and cumulative force. It was an affected, self-conscious performance; the fierce onrush, which should be like that of a river at the spring flood, checked and diverted by an over-desire for finish. It was "faultily faultless," like Tennyson's Maud. A master player will grasp the work in its entirety; while giving the characteristic beauty to each feature, he will have the complete form distinctly present in his mind, so that every passage will be a preparation for that which is to follow and a consequence of that which has gone before. He will also apprehend the essential emotional character of the composition — passionate, merry, languishing, solemn, pathetic, or whatever it may be — and every phrase will receive its proper treatment as a contributing factor in the larger purpose.

Perfection of phrasing might be said to be the supreme sign of mastership, since it is closely united with control of tempo and shading. Furthermore, it implies large executive resources, for if a pianist plays up to the limit of his technique an artistic command of phrasing, nuance, and tempo will surely be wanting. There will be a suggestion of effort, perhaps of strain, and the sign of this, even where no false notes are struck, will be a lack of clearness and freedom in shading and phrasing. But when the performer is able, at any chosen tempo and in spite of every technical difficulty, to present the work in its true emotional atmosphere, luminous in every detail, perfectly articulated and balanced, buoyant with conscious reserve of power, rejoicing in freedom while obedient to law, then the grateful auditor will be ready to confer the degree of artist *summa cum laude.*

In what has been said thus far it may seem that too much stress has been laid upon the player's liberty. But I have thought that a discussion of the art of the pianist from this point of view would be of most value to the music lover who desires to know something of the higher criticism in piano music. There is, of course, another side to the story. The pianist's work is based on laws and principles to which he must submit, however great his genius. It is only after long training and experience that he can be allowed to give loose rein to his own natural impulses. Looming above him, warning and guiding him, is the authority of artistic laws which are as imperative as natural forces. These decrees are final because they are the expression of something inherent in the very constitution of the human mind. Next below these ultimate commands are methods, styles, customs which have acquired the sanction that is drawn from the consensus of the most intelligent practice. As the generations come and go experiments of every conceivable kind are made; certain procedures, not being justified by sober reflection, are abandoned, while others are maintained because in the long run they agree with the matured sense of artistic propriety. Hence arise what are called "traditions." These traditions, however, are not absolutely rigid. There is no finality in art, because where there is mental activity and an insatiable search for truth even the works of the older masters will be seen through an atmosphere created by the temper and experience of the age, and a changed point of view will modify their aspect. The master pianist may say, Why should not I also have a share in the making of tradition? Mendelssohn and other musicians of his time no doubt believed that the tradition of the performance of Beethoven's symphonies was once for all established, but then came Wagner, Liszt, Bülow, Richter and their disciples, and the tradition underwent a change. In piano playing there are capacities for varying beauty in the improved instrument that were undreamed of by Mozart and Beethoven; the performer, therefore, may add color to their works and is not required to preserve the dry light of the old time. The master pianist must hold the balance between two inclinations — one to deny his own instinct toward self-expression and efface himself in presence of the composer, the other to ignore the composer's authority and give free rein to his own egotism.

But what is the proper balance? There indeed is the difficulty. All admit that the player must be true to the spirit and meaning of the composer, but since the composer's intention must be mainly inferred from the composition itself there comes that latitude of interpretation, that exercise of the performer's judgment, taste, and musicianship which gives to piano recitals their perpetual interest. The pianist, like the actor, is a man of his time. Contemporary tendencies in art will show themselves in piano playing as in other fields of expression. Certain general principles, however, stand sure. Mozart must not be played like Tchaikovsky, nor a Beethoven Adagio like a Chopin Nocturne. It is not a question of period, however, as some seem to assert, but of style. A composer of the present who should write like Mozart must be played like Mozart, and not with the contrasts of speed and dynamics that are proper to a Liszt Rhapsodie. But there is a more or less necessary connection between the style of a composer's work and his period; hence the player must be familiar with the history of his art in order that he may be conscious of the background of every typical work, and enter sympathetically into the special character which it may possess as the reflection of the ideals and methods of its age.

There abides the old antithesis between "subjective" and "objective" playing. The subjective player makes the work his own, he discharges through it his own temperament, and he never plays it twice in exactly the same way. The objective player treats the work as external to himself, he aims to perform it, to the best of his knowledge and belief, precisely as the composer would do; he fixes in his memory every dynamic sign, he scrupulously follows the tradition, and he endeavors to play the work in the same manner at every repetition down to the smallest details. Rubinstein said to a pupil, "Play as you feel. Is the day rainy?

Play it in one way. Is it sunny? Play it in another way." A player of the school of Mendelssohn would probably have said: This way, or this, is correct; so must it always be done.

The discussion is of little moment, for strictly speaking there is no such thing as purely subjective or purely objective performance. The happy limitations of our notation system forbid the latter, and as for subjective playing there is only one sort that is completely such, and that is improvising. In former days extemporaneous playing, in which the pianist was composer and executant at the same instant, was the *summum bonum*, the ultimate test of mastership. But in these latter times the pianist gains his crown through his ability as an interpreter of the works of other men. Undoubtedly something has been lost by the change. If we are to trust contemporary report, the unpremeditated performances of Beethoven and Liszt exhibited a splendor, a fire, and an eloquence of appeal that are not paralleled in the deliberate reproductions of the modern method. The gain, however, has more than balanced the loss. A Beethoven or a Liszt appears only once in a generation, while Paderewski and Hofmann and the noble army of their compeers keep ever before us the glorious works of the great tone poets, endowed by the love and the imagination of the interpreter with the magical, ever-renewed charm of re-creation. The master player gives to his performance a glow and an energy as of an improvisation, but he is saved from exaggeration and egotistic straining after originality by a humble deference to the composer and a reverence for the established laws of his art. At the keyboard, under the excitement of the moment and the nervous stimulation that comes from the enthusiasm of his audience, he will often put forth powers unsuspected even by himself, and will produce effects apparently unpremeditated. But, like the wise actor, he will not trust wholly to "the inspiration of the moment," and it will probably appear that these seeming novelties of treatment, these outbreaks of exceptional ardency, are simply the intensifying of effects planned in the study chamber and kindled by the electric contact of the *milieu* and the moment into a splendor which the calm of the practice hours could not anticipate. Under such excitements flashed those impassioned displays of which gray-haired contemporaries of Liszt and Rubinstein speak with bated breath and uplifted eyes.

It appears from this examination of the pianist's art that the music lover has in piano music a very large field for study and a provision for ever increasing delight. He will first look for finished technique — for rapidity, force, and clarity in brilliant work, for singing tone and perfect equipoise of melody and harmony under all circumstances. The shading must be full of variety, balanced and distributed like the lights and darks in a fine painting; the crescendos and diminuendos must rise and fall with majestic ease; there must be fulness without confusion, force without violence, delicacy without weakness; a perfect adaptation of the touch, from the crispest staccato to the sustained clinging legato, to the essential character of the passage; above all and everywhere a faultless drawing of the melodic and rhythmic line, the contour and body of every figure clearly revealed and placed firmly upon the metrical foundation. With all this assumed as an evidence of the technical competence of the player, the question of the truth of his interpretation, never perhaps to be finally settled (since the decision is so much affected by personal preferences), will be submitted to that larger knowledge of the laws of art and of the diverse ideals of the masters which the seeker after critical wisdom will constantly labor to acquire.

CHAPTER VII

THE ART OF SONG: MUSIC AND POETRY

The conscientious lover of music, who wants a prop for his judgments more stable than caprice, encounters certain peculiar difficulties when the art of song is in question. And yet it would seem at first thought that all men might instinctively feel and estimate alike. Singing comes nearer to being universal than any other formal expression of emotion. Every impulse that draws men together in the fraternity of a common need has always chosen melody as the most natural, the most appropriate, and the most efficient means of expressing the consciousness of spiritual solidarity. No other agent is so powerful in stimulating the mental excitement that is the forerunner of action. Political and religious leaders know that song is more effective for their ends than rhetoric. Luther's battle was half won when the people began to sing the hymns of the Reformation. Not less endeared is song as an outlet for the more ideal cravings of the individual heart. Love seems always to imply melody, or at least the tuneful impulse. So natural is the connection here that Darwin was led to believe that the very origin of music is to be found in the love calls of the half-human progenitors of mankind. Among the ancient cultivated nations and in a multitude of instances among the simpler races and lower social grades to-day, poetry and music are inseparable. Song is preëminently the social art. It is the only means of artistic expression that can be employed by a large number of people at the same instant and in the same manner. If my neighbor and I can sing in all sincerity the same songs, then for the time being we have established a close tie between one another; we see into each other's hearts and find there something that makes us brothers.

Out of this universal impulse toward vocal expression, which in ordinary conditions remains crude and rudimentary, a fine art has emerged, and men of genius have put into consummate musical utterance those emotional impulses which had already been crystallized into poetry. Their melodies are then taken from the cold page and transmuted into impassioned sound by men and women who are trained in accordance with refined principles of reproductive art. The sway over our spirits exercised by this twofold creative act is due to our consciousness that these singers are our interpreters as well as interpreters of the composers. Their performances are only the farther stage of a process which begins everywhere in the world when a tender longing desires the relief of utterance, for in the most elaborate development of vocal art there is a ground tone of simple feeling that is understood by every heart that is in tune with nature. From the crooning of a monotonous lullaby by some lowly mother in cabin or wigwam to the splendid display of a Sembrich or a Caruso before applauding thousands there is simply the special development of a general faculty. For this reason, perhaps, the world at large feels a more direct interest in acting and singing than in any other form of artistic exercise. The actor and singer are carrying on activities which have been more or less operative in our own experience. We have all used speech and gesture and have at some time sung, whereas comparatively few have played an instrument, carved, painted, or made verses. The difference is that the professional performance is deliberate and cultivated instead of spontaneous; out of a universal unartistic custom there has been evolved a very exquisite form of specialized art.

It may be that this very nearness to nature may account for the fact that the vast majority of those who frequent theatres and concert halls are quite incapable of an accurate critical judgment upon the performances of actors and vocalists. "Of all the branches of musical performance," says Mr. W. J. Henderson, "singing is that about which the great majority of music lovers know the least. The general public makes very little discrimination between the work of a de Reszke or a Melba and that of a fourth rate Sunday night concert singer who has paid the manager to give her an appearance." Elsewhere Mr. Henderson explains this by saying: "The public is not an expert, never was and never will be. It is idle, careless, and indifferent to the critical questions of art." This diagnosis leaves untouched the deeper question *why* the public is so short-sighted, unconscious of the higher truths in art. The public is indeed ignorant, careless perhaps, but I am sure not altogether indifferent. It applauds what it believes to be good. The gallery god gives boisterous approbation to the most atrocious ranting, not from wanton delight in making a noise, but because from his point of view the performance is right and he has a social duty to perform in encouraging merit.

The ridiculously false judgments to which Mr. Henderson alludes are of course due to ignorance, but there are many ignorances, and the one blindness that explains many other errors, it seems to me, is the failure of the average man to grasp the antithesis between art and nature. That art is art precisely because it is not nature, is a statement that bewilders him. To him the one thing needful in art is imitation. Before a landscape painting he asks, Is it natural? In a portrait he sees no merit except that of superficial likeness. Poetry says nothing to him because it is a non-natural speech which he does not understand, or it interests him in proportion as it comes near to prose. In the drama his warmest approval is given to crude reproduction of actual everyday life. And so in respect to singing, it is to the material, viz., the voice, in its more obvious and sensational qualities, that the average man confines his attention, together with the accessory means of personal appeal, such as the singer's physical charm, presence, or magnetism. He is unobservant of those acquired and specialized elements that give so much pleasure to the connoisseur.

Another reason for the inability of the majority to appreciate fine singing is to be found in the fact that song is a composite art. The voice is used for a twofold purpose, and each of its functions is to some extent unfavorable to the full exercise of the other. That is to say, the voice is a musical instrument capable of giving pleasure by inarticulate sound, like a violin, and it is also a medium for the conveyance of thought by means of words. Sustained musical phrases, with changes of pitch and shading, interfere with distinct enunciation; and on the other hand, the effort at distinct enunciation is unfavorable to the maintenance of pure tone quality and sustained delivery. Song, therefore, is to a certain degree a compromise. Musical sound, whose office is to enchant the ear by its sensuous loveliness, is bound to the service of words imparting definite concepts. The listener's attention is directed to both—the abstract tone for the joy of it, and the pronunciation of the text for the understanding of it. Where two factors, unlike in their psychologic effect, are striving to gain possession of the listener's attention, he often finds that the impression of one or both is imperfect.

Even when the singer employs a foreign language, the dilemma is not evaded, for the listener is perfectly aware that the singer is not articulating meaningless syllables, that the style of the music and the delivery are strongly conditioned by the text, and if he cares for anything besides the mere tickling of his ear he tries to get some intimation of what the performer is singing about. To some extent, in any case, his attention is divided, turned now in one direction now in another, so that the point in which he is least instructed, viz., vocal technique, escapes him, and song as a fine art becomes in his consciousness song as crude auditory sensation or verbal declamation.

So much for the practical difficulties in the immediate art of hearing. They are made more uncertain by being involved in a long debated theoretical question which concerns the whole problem of the relation of tone to text in vocal music. Which is the more important of the two? If one must yield to the other, which shall it be? Does the poetry exist for the sake of the music, or the music for the poetry? How does a decision for either claimant affect the ideal and method of the art of singing? According to his verdict will be the music lover's judgment and appreciation of the vocal art. It is worth while to state the problem with considerable fulness, for it will shed light not only upon singing, but also upon the whole question of vocal music in song, oratorio, church music, and opera.

Among those who give serious attention to vocal music in the capacity of listeners two types of mind appear. There is first the man in whom the love of music *per se* is so paramount that it drives all other considerations into the background; language is only incidental, giving occasion for musical sounds; the listener's pleasure consists in music considered as beautiful tone brilliantly executed, not in music as the bearer of sentiment defined in words. The second type lays emphasis upon literary and dramatic values; to him poetry and action are of supreme consequence; the office of music is to reënforce the power of words as representative of ideas. There are even minds of a cast so predominantly literary that music is an interference, an intruder that gets in the way of verse, and they would reduce music to almost complete subordination. It is well known that Goethe's indifference to the songs of Schubert was the result of a jealousy for the art of poetry; music in his conviction must never be so assertive that the listener's attention would be deflected from the words. Hence he preferred the simple strains of Zelter with their gentle melodies, and the pale harmonies that did no more than furnish a slender support to the voice. William Butler Yeats, the Irish poet, goes even further than Goethe in his protest against the allurements of music. He confesses that there is something about music that he does not like, and he discovered the reason when a friend one day spoke to him some verses, with her fingers lightly passing over a stringed instrument which she held upon her knees. "She spoke to a little tune," says Mr. Yeats, "but it was never singing. A singing note would have spoiled everything." He explains his aversion to ordinary song in this wise: "When I heard anything sung I did not hear the words, or if I did their natural pronunciation was altered, or it was drowned in another music which I did not understand."

This suppression of music in deference to poetry satisfies Mr. Yeats because poetry is his passion, but to minds differently constituted the mere "speaking to a tune" would be extremely tantalizing, because there is just enough of musical suggestion to arouse a desire that is constantly thwarted. In melodrama, which some people, even musicians, esteem, where a reciter employs ordinary speech and a piano or an orchestra performs a richly evolved accompaniment, the antagonism is still more decisive, for there is no pretence at amalgamation. These two devices are merely evasions of the difficulty. What is wanted is a union of poetry and music upon such terms that each shall be allowed a large measure of its natural right, neither completely subjected to the other, both so adjusted in stable equipoise that each shall enhance the pleasure that is derived from its fellow. A unity so perfect as this seems practically impossible to attain. The listener cannot give equal attention to both poetry and music at the same time. Their forms, their methods of action, the faculties engaged in their reception are so unlike that the effort to follow the diction of verse with mind intent on poetic values, interferes with the effort to follow the timbre, form, and rhythm of music with mind alert to musical values.

One of the most interesting details in the history of music is found in the annals of the conflict for supremacy between the two factors in song. In a chant the rhythm of the lines imposes itself upon the tones, and the avowed purpose of the music is to emphasize the text. In the unison Gregorian chant, which constituted the music of the church in the early Middle Ages before part-writing was invented, music was already striving to break loose from its thraldom. The "ornate" or "florid" chant was known in early times, even among the nations of antiquity, the voice on occasion soaring away in a flight of rapid notes on a single vowel — a crude but significant attempt to secure an independent exercise of the musical impulse. With the development of the intricate choral counterpoint of the fourteenth, fifteenth, and sixteenth centuries the demand for musical freedom showed itself in another guise: words were lost and their sense obscured in a tangled web of crossing melodies, and the written notes were often decorated with florid improvised embellishments. Popes and bishops endeavored to repress this tendency and maintain the claims of the sacred text against the musical extravagancies of the theorists and choristers, but with little success. The passion for musical indulgence was too strong to be curbed even by the traditional reverence for the liturgy.

When a reaction came, it was outside the fold of the church. The Florentine inventors of the opera at the close of the sixteenth century, revolting against the obscuration of the word in the harmonic confusions of the church chorus, produced a kind of musical declamation in which music, reduced almost to its lowest terms, served merely to bring the text into clear relief, occasionally employing a more tuneful strain out of deference to the natural behests of the musical ear, but avoiding whatever would disturb the concentration of the mind upon word and action. It seemed to Peri, Caccini, and Cavaliere that the problem of dramatic music was solved, but they did not make sufficient allowance for the musical passion rooted in the Italian heart. The genius of Italy in the seventeenth century was musical, not literary. The triumph of verse over melody was short-lived. Melody was slowly disengaged from the simple dry *stile parlante*, and when it "found itself" in the middle of the century there was an outburst of ecstatic song in the opera houses, and in the churches also, that fairly turned the heads of the gay world of Europe. Italian opera composers and their imitators in every land sprang up by hundreds, and with one accord they surrendered themselves heart and soul to the seductions of the aria. Singers trained to give to this melody all the splendor that can be conferred by delicious voices and the last perfection of technique swarmed in every capital in Europe. All ranks were captivated by the novelty and the voluptuous fascinations of the new art, and the vocal feats and the social triumphs of the great singers read like the tales of romance. Never before or since was any form of art expression so completely the despot of its age.

The effect upon poetry, plot, and action can easily be conjectured. It is difficult to maintain two monarchs in one realm, and music in the giddiness of its success reduced its dramatic partner to a position of abject inferiority. The Italian grand opera, as it waxed on the side of melody and vocalism, waned on the side of plot, character, and action. It became stereotyped into a barren, mechanical formalism. Everything was contrived by the composer and librettist in the interest of the singer purely as virtuoso. The opera came to consist of a score or more of arias with an occasional duet, the whole stitched together by monotonous recitatives. A mechanical plan of three divisions was contrived for this aria, and lines were stretched and words repeated so that the text might fit it, instead of the music growing directly out of the form and meaning of the verse. The composer became the vassal of the singer; his mission was not so much to write fine music as it was to contrive musical formulas that would be favorable to the display of the vocal art of this or that popular favorite. The singer had the right to take whatever liberty with these melodies his fancy or conceit suggested, substituting favorable for unfavorable vowels, interpolating the most astonishing flourishes and cadenzas at every opportune or inopportune moment. It must not be supposed that there was no thought of expression on the part of these magnates of the opera. They were praised for pathos as well as for brilliancy, and we know that timbre and truth of shading were considered in the schools as well as volubility of throat and strength of lungs. But poetry in the opera had grown so weak that the sentiments to be expressed became conventionalized; words were little valued except as affording a suggestion for music; very little of natural truth remained in these cold and artificial pretences at musical dramas.

In such conditions the playwright found no inspiration, and he contrived his scenes and verses simply in order that he might provide the number of arias that the "laws" of the opera required. The public became connoisseurs of vocal art as the public is not to-day. Criticism was expended only on quality of voice and execution, and woe to the singer who transgressed the canons of technique in the slightest particular — no truth of action or fine feeling for poetic sentiment could save him from the wrath of his outraged patrons.

This tendency toward an exaggerated specialization, exquisite as its results often were in their impression on the senses, could not hold the favor of those who demanded in art truth to the deeper facts of life and the satisfaction of the intellect, and even in the heyday of its glory the Italian ideal of song met vigorous opposition. Satirists derided the hollow pretension of the opera stage. The French grand opera, founded fifty years after the Italian, although it had its own conventions and artificialities, maintained variety of action, pure declamation, and respect for the written word as cardinal principles, and gave the dance and chorus a prominent place in the dramatic scheme. The opera buffa and the opéra-comique took their characters from contemporary life and insisted upon comic talent, interesting situation, and lively portrayal of homespun sentiment. Handel's oratorios which soon after 1740 took the place of the threadbare Italian opera in the regard of the British public, gave worthy expression to the grandest ideas, and worked directly and indirectly to elevate the standards of taste in respect to both subject and treatment. Then came the reforms of Gluck between 1760 and 1780, based on the endeavor, as he expressed it in his preface to "Alceste," "to reduce music to its proper function, that of seconding poetry by enforcing the expression of the sentiment and the interest of the situation, without interrupting the action or weakening it by superfluous ornament"; setting "no value on novelty as such unless it was naturally suggested by the situation and suited to the expression." The influence of these precepts, uniting with a powerful dramatic instinct, was seen in Mozart's later operas. Beethoven wrote "Fidelio" in order to glorify womanly devotion, and made it his first aim to embellish his theme with all his immense resources of musical expression. Weber and Spohr in Germany, Cherubini, Spontini, Mehul, and Meyerbeer in France, held aloft, in spite of occasional wavering, the standard of Gluck's principles. A reaction toward "the tyranny of the singer" appeared in the brilliant group of Italian composers in the early part of the nineteenth century, of whom Rossini, Bellini, Donizetti, and the young Verdi were chief,—but this reaction was not complete, for these men, although they revived the ancient glories of Italian *bel canto* and were willing enough to sacrifice poetic value and dramatic truth to vocal display if the two ideals ever came into conflict, often sought to reconcile them, and we ought to acknowledge that they really believed, although in a rather unintelligent way, that the things their characters said and did were worth saying and doing, and that their music on the whole possessed fitness as well as sensuous beauty.

The evident conviction on the part of the later Italian and French masters, that poetry and plot had received all the consideration they were entitled to in such a form of art as the opera, might have been accepted by the world if the overwhelming personality of Wagner had not appeared, declaring himself commissioned to destroy the Italian superstition and to fulfil the incomplete tendencies that he found in the better class of French and German opera. Not content with demanding an equilibrium of forces, he bluntly maintained that music must yield to poetry and action. In his most elaborate confession of faith, *Opera and Drama*, he lays down, as the rock basis of his reform, the maxim that the radical error of the opera had always been in making musical effect the end and the drama the means, whereas in a true musical drama the poetic element should be the end and the music the means. It would be easy to show that Wagner was often inconsistent, and that in many passages in his dramas the commanding impression is just as much a one-sided musical effect as it is in any work of his "erroneous" predecessors. In such scenes, for example, as the "fire charm," Brünnhilde's awakening, the following duet between Brünnhilde and Siegfried, the sword forging, Siegfried's dirge, Isolde's death song, and the quintet, "prize song," and final chorus in "The Mastersingers," there is no apparent effort to make the drama the end and the music merely a means. The difference between Wagner and his rivals in such situations is a difference in sheer musical inventive power and a radical difference in form.

One recent composer at least, viz., Debussy in "Pelléas and Melisande," has succeeded in executing Wagner's avowed intention with what may be called complete consistency. That is to say, that the music, however beautiful, is so thoroughly the enveloping atmosphere of the play that the listener is never turned by the sounds of voices and instruments from his concentration upon the action.

In this remarkable work there is the most perfect blend and fusion of scene, poetry, and music that has yet been accomplished except in a few isolated moments in Wagner's work. But is this the final solution of the problem? Is this the complete and perfect music-drama for which the world has been waiting, as Debussy's disciples affirm? Other critics complain that this work lacks musical interest. In this controversy we are landed again upon the old debatable ground. Why, it is asked, should the musical interest be sacrificed, or even subordinated, to the dramatic? May not Wagner's principle, when carried to its farthest consequence, be wrong, and did he not do well to be inconsistent when his inconsistency gave us the most magnificent, the most profoundly emotional music that ever issued from the human brain? Why should people be censured if they go to the opera for musical enjoyment rather than for the gratification of a taste for poetry and action, as unquestionably the vast majority of them do? Is not opera rightly to be classed as a phase of musical art rather than a phase of literary art? Debussy's work is so far an interesting exception to the rule, and there is no sign that the public will ever treat the opera as a mere substitute for the spoken drama. Nevertheless, the work of Gluck and Mozart and Wagner and the later Verdi has not been in vain. The opera will never relapse to its former condition in which poetic subject was a matter of indifference and the actor was lost in the singer. Time has accomplished its revenges for violations of truth; the operas that have survived their generation and are established in the esteem of thoughtful minds have been those that are strong on the dramatic side.

The war between word and tone has also been fought out with equal lack of conclusiveness in the domain of lyric song. But in this field the sacrifice of poetic interest to vocal display has never gone to such lengths as in the opera. Indeed the instances have been comparatively rare in which either lyric composers or lyric singers have been content to treat the voice merely as an apparatus for sensational virtuosity. Such an abuse can hardly exist when any heed is given to literary merit in the selection of verse for musical setting, and the fact has been that the best song composers have as a rule chosen poems that possess beauty in thought and diction, and have written music not simply for the sake of independent melodious charm, but rather with an eye to the appropriate expression of the text. The reason for this difference between song and the opera is perfectly clear. The lyric poets do not commonly write their verses simply for the musicians to make songs of; the poetry, however it may seem to invite musical treatment, is intended to stand alone, and thus having no end beyond itself it is the expression of the best skill of the author. The opera libretto, on the contrary, is never planned to make an independent impression; the writer's purpose is not to produce a literary and dramatic work of self-dependent interest, but a more or less mechanical verbal contrivance that will be adapted to the special exigencies of scenic and musical effect according to theatrical conventions. Librettists as a rule are not poets "by the grace of God," but clever adapters of scenes, mechanical artificers of verse, whose aim is not literary but musical effect. The opera composer rarely finds a dramatic poem that can be used as it stands, he must have one built for him out of new or old material. The song writer, on the contrary, is never at a loss for a text; the world is full of beautiful poetry waiting, without the slightest need of alteration, for his use. There is no excuse for him if he chooses verse of inferior quality; and when he has taken his text, if he has in him the love of poetry (and if he has not he does not deserve to be called a song writer at all) he treats it with veneration, and makes it his dearest hope that he may be able to do something worthy of the noble art to which he has joined his own.

It is the spirit of church music and the folk song that has been transmitted to the lyric art song, not the spirit of the opera. The very conception, method, and environment of the opera, with its elaborate machinery, its combination of mediums—scenery, action, vocal music, orchestral music—its necessity for instantaneous and stirring effect, all encourage spectacularism. The finer shades of emotion, the more tender communing of mind with mind, require the more delicate vehicle of the lyric. The opera has always been the favorite entertainment of a limited number, not to say of a separate caste; the music of the people has been church music and lyric song. The Greeks knew the subtle affinity that draws music into the embrace of poetry; the Minnesingers and Troubadours knew it; in the Elizabethan age this mutual passion was recognized and blessed. But not until the nineteenth century has this wedlock been crowned with an offspring that perpetuates the dual strength and loveliness of its parentage. The age of the great German song composers was coincident with the revival of lyric poetry under the hands of Goethe, Schiller, and the romanticists. In fact, it lies in the nature of the case that in this branch of musical art the composers wait upon the poets, the musicians finding little inspiration in prosaic and commonplace verse. Another striking illustration is the rise of the brilliant group of French song composers of the last half century, following the outburst of French lyric poetry begun in the works of André Chenier and continued in Lamartine, Victor Hugo, De Musset, Gautier, Alfred de Vigny, Leconte de Lisle, Verlaine, and their compeers. Schubert, who leads the brilliant host of modern song writers, exemplifies the controlling tendency of his school by seeking his texts among the works of such men as Goethe, Schiller, Heine, Shakespeare, Scott, and the poets of his day and country who expressed, although with varying ability, the genuine emotions of the common heart. This guiding motive was adopted by his successors, and so stimulating was this ideal to the inventive powers of every musician who had accepted truth to the inner life of the soul as the law of his art, that the lyric inspiration swept like a spiritual trade wind over the world, and Schumann, Franz, Brahms, Jensen, and Wolf found worthy emulators in the Norwegians Grieg and Kjerulf, the Russians Rubinstein and Tchaikovsky, the Hungarian Liszt, the Bohemian Dvořák, the American MacDowell, and the Frenchmen Fauré, Godard, Duparc, Saint-Saëns, Massenet, and Debussy. These composers, with many others hardly less worthy of esteem, have discovered an art in which music and poetry penetrate one another in a mingling so complete that each word finds an inevitable correlative in a musical tone, poetic line and musical phrase twinborn, mutually dependent and inseparable. Every lover of song has in his memory scores of lyrics of which it might be said that music has not so much added a new means of expression to verse as it has drawn forth an emotion which words can but partly reveal, and endowed poetic utterance with a new attribute.

In this union the poetry remains the motive power determining the course of the composer's invention. His purpose is not, as in former periods, to produce something that is in and of itself musically pleasing, but rather, taking possession of verse in which genuine human feeling is appropriately rendered, to fashion such a setting for this jewel that the most subtle refinements of poetic suggestion shall find their convincing counterpart in musical chord or phrase. Vocal music thus declares its correspondence with what is perhaps the most productive tendency in nineteenth century art, viz., direct, truthful characterization. Absolute fitness of style is the demand, the most subtle and direct interpretation, even though formal beauty and superficial sensuous charm be sacrificed.

The most eminent exponent of this tendency in opera is, of course, Richard Wagner. He is likewise an eloquent champion of it in his critical and autobiographical writings. No plainer statement of this principle and its consequences in the composition of melody could be made than that of Wagner, in *A Communication to My Friends.* If the reader will refer back to what has been said in the section on melody in this book, Wagner's statement will be clear. "Wherever," he says, "I had to give utterance to the emotions of my *dramatis personæ*, as shown by them in feeling discourse, I was forced entirely to abstain from this rhythmic melody of the Folk [that is, the conventional structure of four and eight measure metre]: or rather, it could not occur to me to employ that method of expression; nay, here the dialogue itself, conformably to the emotional contents, was to be rendered in such a fashion that, *not the melodic Expression, per se, but the expressed Emotion* should rouse the interest of the hearer. The melody must therefore spring, quite of itself, from out the verse; in itself, as sheer melody, it could not be permitted to attract attention, but only in so far as it was the most expressive vehicle for an emotion already plainly outlined in the words. With this strict conception of the melodic element, I now completely left the usual operatic mode of composition; inasmuch as I no longer tried intentionally for customary melody, or, in a sense, for Melody at all, but absolutely *let it take its rise* from feeling utterance of the words." [1]

In judging the merits of this later style of "continuous music" as applied to song and opera, one must recognize the difference between the idea of a lyric poem and that of a dramatic scene. There are, indeed, varieties of lyrics, but the strict definition of such a poem is that it presents a single thought or sentiment, permitting its phrases to alter in changing circumstances, allowing the thought to reveal new aspects under varying lights, letting the fancy play around it, yet essentially *one* mood, *one* conception, not describing the events that produced the feeling or anticipating its consequences, but a direct immediate presentation of the feeling itself, with just enough of incident to localize and determine the feeling and bring it into relief. When the mood has been set forth in a clear and appealing way the purpose of the poem is accomplished. Hence in a multitude of lyrics suitable for musical setting the old form of tune, returning upon itself, leading back to its first strain and its first key, even repeating the tune note

[1] Translation by William Ashton Ellis.

for note in the successive stanzas, is perfectly appropriate. Schubert was not in error as to his form when he wrote "Who is Sylvia?" and "Faith in Spring." The treatment in these songs is as proper as the quite different method in "The Phantom Double" and "The Erl King." Even in the opera the conventional song form may still be admissible where the action becomes stationary and the actor expresses a feeling that requires a considerable amount of time for its unfolding. Delila's song, "My Heart at Thy Sweet Voice," in Saint-Saëns's "Samson and Delila" is not to be condemned on any just principle of musico-dramatic propriety. But in the large stretches of an opera scene the present-day insistence upon dramatic truth accepts Wagner's principle with certain modifications. In a true drama there must be constant life, change, and movement; a frequent arrest for the sake of vocal display leads inevitably to the old abuses. With the reassertion of dramatic reality and poetic interest the form becomes more continuous, expansive, and flexible, and the enforcement of the law that musical form must grow inevitably out of the matrix of the verse compels formalism to give way to direct and intimate expression.

All the musical forms that ever existed are, it seems to me, still valid. Their justification, however, rests upon their fitness to the thought, verse diction, or situation which calls them into life. Even the colorature song, which composers no longer write, is often able to vindicate its reason for being. Even Wagner speaks of "the classic nobleness of the Italian vocal art of earlier times." But the former acquiescence in musical charm at the cost of truth was a sign of an imperfect criterion of judgment. Another, which we believe to be higher, has taken its place.

The effect of the new principle and method in lyric and dramatic music upon the vocalist can easily be understood. The singer who adopts the interpretative conception accepts the sovereignty of poetry and makes the expression of the poet's mind the end and aim of his effort. He feels the poetry through and through. He studies it as the actor studies his lines. His vocal style, his tone color, his determination of speed and dynamics, his phrasing — all issue from the endeavor to keep the thought of the text uppermost in his mind. In the singing of a typical artist of this school there are three creative personalities in alliance for one common end; poet, composer, and singer are actuated by a single purpose, and the listener finds that his attention is not wandering in a maze of distracting sounds, but directed along the path marked out by the poet's imagination.

The music lover will now naturally ask if the two ideals presented in the history of song — perfect vocal technique as an end in itself, and supreme emphasis upon poetic expression — are compatible with one another. Need there be conflict between them? Does insistence upon the most refined vocalism involve any sacrifice of truth of pronunciation and poetic emphasis, or may impurity of voice or flaws in execution be excused in return for perfect declamation and strong intellectual and emotional conception? There are certainly conspicuous instances in which one has been exalted over the other, and singers of both types have had enthusiastic admirers. The consummate flower of the Italian *bel canto* has been displayed in later days in the singing of Adelina Patti. Mr. Henry T. Finck says of her: "Niemann was no doubt right in pronouncing her the most perfect vocalist of all times." "The ordinary epithets applicable to a voice, such as sweet, sympathetic, flexible, expressive, sound almost too commonplace to be applied to Patti's voice at its best." "Her voice has a natural sensuous charm like a Cremona violin, which it is a pleasure to listen to irrespective of what she happens to be singing. It is a pleasure, too, to hear under what perfect control she has it; how, without changing the quality of the sound, she passes from a high to a low note, from piano to forte, gradually or suddenly, and all without the least sense of effort. Indeed her notes are as spontaneous as those of a nightingale." In later years she showed more and more anxiety to win renown as a dramatic singer, and here, Mr. Finck says, "the vocal style which she exclusively cultivated proved an insuperable obstacle. Although free from the smaller vices of the Italian school, she could not overcome the great and fatal shortcoming of that school — the maltreatment of the poetic text. She could not find the proper accents required in operas where the words of the text are as important as the melody itself. Having neglected to master the more vigorous vowels and expressive consonants, she cannot assert her art in dramatic works. Her voice, in short, is merely an instrument."

As a conspicuous example of a singer of the opposite kind we have had in recent years Dr. Ludwig Wüllner, who was advertised at his first appearance in this country as "a great singer without a voice." Here was a rather startling challenge to established notions of the vocal art. Dr. Wüllner has in a high degree the abilities of an actor. His literary knowledge is extensive and his taste that of a man of broad culture. He can enter sympathetically into a very wide range of poetic conceptions. In articulation, pronunciation, emphasis, variety of expression, mastery of all the nuances of feeling — boisterous humor, tenderness, pathos, and grimmest tragedy — flexibility in adaptation of style to subject, accumulative force in working up emotional climaxes — in all these features his truthfulness of conception (barring an occasional tendency to exaggerate) and vividness of presentation are extraordinary, and the impression he produced has had few parallels in the annals of music in America. The first enthusiasm beginning to abate, voices of protest were heard. High critical authorities declared that the art of pure song had rights which this great musical declaimer constantly violated; that his voice lacking sensuous charm, and his method betraying indifference to the classic laws which the acknowledged masters of three centuries had promulgated, he was undoing the work of earnest and conservative vocal teachers, and misleading the critical judgment of the public into the belief that bad intonation, harshness of tone, and lack of all the vocal graces are matters of little consequence provided that "expression," especially "dramatic expression," is assured. Is singing, the objectors ask, the rendering of poetry by means of tones that are charming to the ear under all circumstances, or is it a matter of accents and tempos and dynamics with merely rhetorical ends in view, unregardful of the laws of musical beauty and perfection which have hitherto been maintained in vocal and instrumental music alike?

The musical public seems to be divided upon this issue. In every country vocal sins are perpetrated by distinguished performers and pardoned in the interest of what is called "interpretation." On the other hand, many frequenters of operas and concerts — probably the majority — are heedless of all considerations except purity, brilliancy, or flexibility of voice. Madame Patti and Dr. Wüllner have both had their unqualified admirers; and yet reason and experience would seem to declare that neither affords the model to which the earnest singer should aspire. Beautiful singing is not wholly poetic expression, for the voice is an instrument on which one plays for the delight of the ear. Neither is it pure tone and finished technique wholly, for without uncovering the soul that dwells in poetry it cannot move the intellect. Both qualities — emotional expression and technical completeness — may unite, and there is no inherent reason why they should not supplement and sustain each other. It is no doubt true that in the lyric drama and German Lied there has been in some quarters a disregard of vocal perfection as a result of reaction against the one-sidedness of the old Italian school, but no considerable portion of the world will ever be content with bad singing under any pretence. Another reaction is now in progress, the nature of which is shown by the assertion that is becoming frequent among the best writers, that there is but one right way to sing, whether the music be that of Mozart, Handel, Schubert, or Wagner. Harshness of tone, a jerky explosive style, an audible gasp when taking breath, a perpetual unsteadiness, a lazy sliding from note to note — these vices are not expressive, and are no more to be indulged in the modern declamatory music than in the classic *bel canto*. This law finds no obstacle to its enforcement in the fact that composers nowadays aim more at writing music that is characteristic than music that is formally beautiful in the classic sense. Emphasis may shift from one side to another, and composers may risk audacities of expression from which their forbears would shrink in dismay; nevertheless, singing remains an art and cannot survive unless it obeys the universal laws of its kingdom. Just as a drama so naturalistic that the time-honored principles of acting must be abolished would not be good art; just as a painting so literally imitative that the criteria of draftsmanship and composition that have been maintained by every master from the beginning are defied, would not be good art; so any alliance of poetry and music for ends whose realization would put ugliness of sound in place of beauty would be self-destructive. No art is expected always to remain isolated and solitary; the arts may combine for purposes which one alone cannot accomplish; but in this union they are not required to deny their original natures, they must still remain capable of giving separately that special and peculiar pleasure for which they were individually endowed.

CHAPTER VIII

THE ART OF SONG: THE TECHNIQUE OF THE SINGER

THERE need be no quarrel with the assertion that the end and aim of technique is expression. Pure vocalism, however, is not merely a means. A lovely voice, perfectly controlled, is in itself a cause of happiness not to be repented of, even leaving out of the account its relation to words. Lyric and dramatic interpretation and trained mechanism need never be set over against one another as divergent in aim, and they should not be separated in the consciousness of the singer or hearer. Nevertheless, there is so marked a tendency in certain quarters to disregard the classic traditions of refined voice production in the supposed interest of "expression" that it seems worth while to devote a short chapter to the technical principles involved in good singing. There is all the more reason for this in the fact that the great majority of music lovers are so ignorant of what constitutes correct singing that when they hear a voice which gives an excitement to their nerves by its sensuous quality, especially by its brilliancy or power, they applaud and go away satisfied, indifferent to many faults or merits which an intelligent critic condemns or praises.

An appreciation of skill in singing is certainly a necessary part of a music lover's education. The principles involved are so few and so easily stated that no one need mistake them. As this book is not a technical treatise on any branch of musical art, but an attempt to show the amateur how and where to direct his observation, a brief enumeration seems to be all that is required.

The laws of good vocalism which it is needful to bear in mind may be placed in two categories, one including the proper production and management of tone, the other dealing with suitableness of style to the sentiment of the text. In the first case the laws are essentially the same as those that are involved in the playing of instruments in which sustained tones capable of shading are produced, such as the violin, clarinet, or horn. Up to a certain point the critical listener will be safe in his judgments if he compares a singer's execution with that of a violinist. In fact, a singer, as well as a lover of singing, can learn much by listening to fine violin playing.

In the first place, the hearer will expect that the tones of the singer's voice will be pure and agreeable. One would suppose that there need be no mistake on this point, but every critic has noticed the singular fact that a voice will often sound neutral or even unpleasant to one ear and beautiful to another. In such cases prejudice or some kind of accessory or association will have a good deal to do — friendship perhaps, or admiration for a singer's mental or moral qualities, strongly affecting the impression made upon the ear. Such questions as this, however, may be left out of the account. I shall assume that sensuously beautiful tones are immediately appreciated by people with a normal auditory apparatus. The warning that is required must be addressed to those who perceive voice quality and nothing else.

It is not surprising that where physical beauty of tone exists it should often drive all other considerations out of the field. There is no other sensation received by ear or eye that is capable of giving quite that thrill of rapture that is felt when the nerves of hearing are swept by a flood of glorious tones issuing from the throat of a great singer. One's whole frame seems to quiver in sympathetic vibration. This extraordinary effect is not merely physical; it is also psychological. It is "the cry of the human," and it is the deepest soul in us that makes reply. We call a lovely voice "sympathetic," and there is a world of associations involved in that word, some near, some remote, passing down to us through uncounted generations that have aspired, suffered, and enjoyed. The ecstasy kindled by an entrancing voice has a source deeper than we know. Its communications are beyond all measure subtle and extended. It is the admonition of the higher instincts, it is a visitation that redeems us for the moment from the thraldom of space and time. Individual interests give way to those that are common and universal. No one need apologize if his nature responds with whole-hearted enthusiasm to such an appeal as this.

A voice capable of producing such effects through its timbre alone is rare, and even such a voice is to a large degree dependent upon certain powers that are not native but acquired — accomplishments that are secured only by prolonged and intelligent labor. This art, like every other, is built upon science. The proper emission and control of tone, without which natural gifts are of no avail, are attainments that are deliberate, self-conscious, and to a large extent mechanical. They are mastered only after years of assiduous study under the direction of wise and experienced teachers. These acquired technical habitudes enter into the account in a listener's enjoyment, whether he is fully conscious of the fact or not, and, as in all appreciation of art, a knowledge of the problems and the difficulties involved has much to do with his satisfactions. A little instruction shows him that good singing, merely on the side of tone production, is not a simple matter, and that it is well for him to acquire certain other perceptions besides his unreflective recoil to the mere physical impact of sound.

The first necessity in fine singing is that the tones shall be true in intonation, that is to say, the voice must be exactly on the pitch in every note, and every tone must be carried through without the slightest wavering, whether the notes be long or short, loud or soft, high or low, and whether the passage be quick or slow, shaded or uniform. To the average listener a voice will seem beautiful if the intonation is perfect, although it may be quite ordinary so far as timbre is concerned. This perfect accuracy of pitch and firmness of tone, which is in itself very agreeable and seems to make other virtues possible, ought, we think, to be a matter of course. Just here, however, appears the very singular fact that singing out of tune and singing with an unsteady flow of sound are not uncommon on the dramatic and concert stage, that famous singers are often guilty of one or both faults, and that many audiences appear not to be offended thereby. There have, indeed, been times when singers actually cultivated the tremolo, and audiences accepted it as a new beauty that had come as a blessing into the world. The tremolo, it is said, became the fashion in Paris, and afterward in other musical centres, because it was employed by Rubini, the most adored tenor of the first part of the nineteenth century, in his later years to conceal the deterioration of his organ. In this singular fact we have an illustration of a prevalent trait in human nature. "It is only a few years ago," says the English anthropologist, Edward Clodd, "when a royal personage had an affection of the knee which caused her to walk lame, that 'society' affected what was called the 'Alexandra limp.'" As beautiful as a limp is in walking, so is the tremolo in singing.

People have tried to defend the tremolo against the strictures of the judicious on the ground that as 'cello players employ it persistently it ought to be equally permitted to singers. But the vocal tremolo and the quivering of a string under the finger of a 'cellist are not the same thing. The player keeps his finger on the same spot and his vibrato is without change of pitch. If he slid his finger up and down the string while making it tremble, the effect would be similar to the tremolo of a singer and would be thoroughly reprehensible. A vibrato effect may sometimes be employed by a singer in an intensely emotional situation, but only exceptionally. A persistent "wobble" is as much out-of-tune singing as persistent flatting. It is even worse, for flatting has the merit of consistency at least, and may be due to temporary conditions for which the singer is not wholly to blame. A confirmed tremolo is a nerveless, spineless, debilitated thing, a mark of infirmity and a frequent forerunner of collapse. It is due to physical weakness or false vocal method. It is never to be approved, but sternly condemned or charitably pitied.

The great secret of a tone that is always steady, always pure, always true, is in the management of the breath. A discussion of the proper method of breathing does not belong here; indeed, the listener should not be reminded that breath is being taken, except as noble tone and masterly phrasing lead his curiosity back into the causes of these beauties. There must be no hitching up of the shoulders when the lungs are filled, no audible aspiration at the attack, no breathiness in the sound, no escaping air from the lungs that is not turned into tone. The hearer must be allowed to forget that the singer is a human being with a limited lung capacity; the breath must be taken secretly, and its volume so sustained that the singing will give an impression of exhaustless resources, like the rising and falling of the breeze on a summer's day.

Wagner's maxim, already quoted, that "the tone sustained with equal power is the basis of all expression," applies with as much force to singing as to orchestral playing. The fundamentals of the method taught by the old Italian masters, says Mr. W. J. Henderson, were "the pure legato and sonorous, beautiful tone." It was said by a contemporary of Rubini in his prime that this great singer "can so control his breath as never to expend more of it than is absolutely necessary for producing the exact degree of sound he wishes. So adroitly does he conceal the artifice of respiration that it is impossible to discover when his breath renews itself, inspiration and expiration being apparently simultaneous, as if one were to fill a cup with one hand while emptying it with the other." Seek the round pure tone and the firm legato, it may be said to vocal students, and all other graces shall be added unto you. The critical listener, at any rate, should be content with nothing less.

Not only should this control of tone be equally evident in all parts of the voice from the lowest note to the highest, but the quality of tone should be virtually the same throughout the singer's compass. This reads like a counsel of perfection; a literal enforcement of it might seem oppressive; the critic must be charitable. Absolute similarity of sound from one extreme of pitch to another does not exist in the case of any orchestral instrument, and it seems rather too much to demand it literally of the human throat. There are singers, justly recognized as great, whose voices change somewhat in character in different parts of their range. Rarely, if ever, does nature give equality in timbre and volume as a primary endowment. Somewhere in the voice occurs the natural "break," above which the novice finds a constriction, as though the vocal chords were squeezed together in order to resist all further upward progress. We need not enter into the vexed question of "registers," over which vocal teachers have so long disputed with an unbecoming acrimony; it is enough to say that in almost every voice there is at least one point where the tones tend to become weak and veiled, and beyond that point to undergo a change in quality. It is the teacher's business to remove this obstacle and so train the tone delivery that the broken instrument shall be mended and the transition from one part of the voice to another made smooth and open. The perfect singer will not give the impression that there are two or three voices in the throat, but only one. Where the triumph over nature is complete the effect may be compared to the playing of a passage of two octaves or so upon a single violin string. More commonly, however, among good singers the effect is more analogous to playing on all the strings of a violin. There is an appreciable difference between the G and E strings, but the tone is always the string tone. It is quite possible that a voice perfectly uniform in quality throughout, if such a voice could exist, would be somewhat cold and monotonous, lacking the power of changing the color for expressional needs. The demand, therefore, is especially that the voice be equally pure and under control everywhere, passing from one region to another without apparent effort, always maintaining suppleness, steadiness, and accuracy of intonation.

In good singing each tone will begin exactly on the proper pitch without any sliding or groping after the tone, and the tone will be round and firm from the very first instant. The beginning of a tone is called the attack. With a good attack the tone sounds as if it had been already formed in its perfection and were only waiting to be set free. There is no suggestion of timidity or uncertainty. There is none of the aspirated or clucking sound at the beginning of a phrase such as one often hears in imperfect vocalism. A good attack is like the prompt opening of an organ pipe; there are no premonitory symptoms of tone, no unmusical instant, however brief; the tone fully formed leaps into being, round, buoyant, pellucid like the drops that spring from a fountain.

And as tones and phrases begin so should they end. The tone vanishes not as if the breath were exhausted; it does not slide or tremble into extinction, but the impulsion of breath is suddenly withdrawn and the tone instantly ceases while still in its perfection. It makes no difference in what part of the voice the tone may be, upon what vowel or consonant it may be engaged, whether it is loud or soft, or what may be the nature of the expression — the tone must be perfectly formed and perfectly controlled at its inception and its close. Perfect attack and finish are very beautiful to hear, and they imply many things that are highly creditable to the performer.

With proper tone formation, perfect breath control, accurate attack and release, and the easy blending of the registers once acquired, the singer should be able to maintain accuracy in these particulars through all the innumerable degrees and transitions of force and speed upon which variety and truth of expression depend. One of the most beautiful effects in music is the "swell," the increase and diminishing of a tone by imperceptible gradations. It may be compared to a perfect curve in drawing — a beautiful thing in itself aside from any ulterior purpose of expression or design. It gives to the voice and to stringed and wind instruments a means of pleasure which instruments like the piano and harp do not afford, and which even the organ cannot give except by a sort of subterfuge. This ornament, as employed in singing, is technically known as the *messa di voce*. It is one of the final evidences of the singer's command of his instrument. Let a vocalist begin a tone softly, with a perfect attack, enlarge it to full volume so gradually that the listener cannot distinguish the successive instants of increase because there are none, any more than there are straight lines in a circle; then let the singer reduce the sound by the same inappreciable gradations until it seems to taper to a point and vanish, one hardly knows when — all without the least suspicion of wavering or change of quality — and we have one of the most delectable effects that the vocal art can offer. In successions of notes or phrases we may have the same mastery of nuance, and with it the song attains life, freedom, warmth, and color.

Agility and power in a high degree are demanded in certain kinds of music, but as they are not required in all they are not to be accounted indispensable, like the qualities that have just been mentioned. The vocalists that have been most adored by the great public, however, have been those that excelled in brilliancy and force. The multitude enjoys most whatever appeals to the raw nervous susceptibility, and among all the sensations that enrapture the senses and heat the blood few can compare with the feats of agility for which the kings and queens of song in the golden days of *bel canto* were celebrated. A cool person in a theatre when a Catalani, a Farinelli, or a Tètrazzini had broken melody into a dazzling shower of coruscations might be excused for believing that the audience had suddenly been transformed into a horde of maniacs. When one looks at the records in print of some of the cadenzas delivered by the singers of the florid school, one can faintly imagine the effect upon the auditory nerves when these passages were shaken forth upon the air by such a voluptuous organ as that of a Jenny Lind or an Adelina Patti. Aside from the sensuous quality of tone, these acrobatic vocal feats gratify the universal love of the marvelous, exciting the admiration that every one feels in the presence of some supremely skilful triumph over difficulties. It is said that Rossi, a famous singer of the seventeenth century, could sing a chromatic trill chain of two octaves up and down again, all in one breath. Farinelli, of the eighteenth century, vanquished a noted trumpet player in a public contest, surpassing his rival in power and in rapidity of utterance. Thomas Ryan, in his *Recollections of an Old Musician*, tells of a cadenza composed by Julius Benedict for Jenny Lind, to be sung by the "Swedish Nightingale" at the end of a cavatina. "The cadenza was sung without accompaniment; it covered two pages of music paper, and was written in a style suited to an instrumental concerto. Toward the end there was a sequence of ascending and descending arpeggios of diminished sevenths, which flowed into a scale of trills from a low note to one of her highest; then dwelling very long on that note and trilling on it, she gradually returned to the theme of the cavatina, when it was perceived that her wonderfully fine musical ear had unerringly guided her through the mazes of the long cadenza and brought her to the tonic note of the piece with surprising correctness of intonation."

It is not wise wholly to disdain these marvels of laryngeal virtuosity as though they were of the same grade of value as the feats of Japanese gymnasts. Trills, runs, skips, and staccatos, when combined with varied tone colors, accents, changes in volume and rate of speed, may have an expressive purpose as well as a decorative charm. It is a noticeable fact, however, that while the popular love of ornamental singing seems to be as strong as ever and an accomplished exponent of "coloratures" will still excite a prodigious furore, nevertheless the composers who furnish the material for it are wholly of the past, and the Tetrazzini type of singer must fall back upon the threadbare operas of the Italian and French composers of the early part of the nineteenth century. Mr. Henry T. Finck speaks of this interesting fact as a "mystery." "Why," he asks, "have the composers of all countries given up writing florid music when the public at large evidently likes it better than anything else, demands it with applausive violence and showers diamonds on the Pattis and Sembrichs, the Melbas and Tetrazzinis who provide it?" He goes on to show that not only the German and French opera composers, but also the composers of Italy, where florid song had its birth and its richest bloom, have given it up completely.

This failure of the composers to give the public what it craves does seem at first thought a little puzzling, but it is not the first time in the history of art that artists have chosen to obey the higher laws rather than seek notoriety and emolument by catering to the whim of the sensation-loving populace. The composers of the last half of the nineteenth century have seen a great light, and they have nobly chosen to "follow the gleam." Moreover there is no credit to a musician in writing florid cadenzas. Nothing is easier. They require no skill. Anybody who knows one key from another can do the trick. And further, in these colorature arias of the old school the composer is obliged to withdraw into the shade, while the singer flourishes in the full glare of the lime light. No composer who respects himself and his art will willingly take such a humiliating position of subordination. "The old order changeth, yielding place to new." The style of music brought into vogue by Wagner and his successors, driving out the obvious tunes and the conventional vocal embroideries of the Rossini-Bellini–Donizetti school, has lifted the composer to his rightful station, and now, secure of his position, he refuses longer to sacrifice himself to the honor and glory of the limber throated vocalist. All this, perhaps, may serve as a partial solution of the "mystery."

The study of colorature song, in spite of its abuses, is of advantage to every singer, for the practice of it promotes flexibility and control. A vocalist who is skilled in it has a voice that is under subjection for all kinds of music, just as a pianist needs highly developed fingers for the sake of equality of touch and perfect command of shading even where technical demands are moderate. The singer should give the impression of ease and security at all times, no indication of effort should appear no matter how difficult the passage, and in every phrase each note must be as distinct as it is in the playing of an Ysaye or a Godowski. Besides this, florid music is not out of date, nor will it ever be, even though composers have abandoned it. The singing of Handel and Mozart requires a voice exceedingly supple and fluent, and Handel and Mozart stand among the immortal masters of song. The listener will demand that all music of whatever type shall be sung with a clear-cut delivery of every note; that a chromatic scale shall be a succession of plainly distinguishable half-steps and not a portamento slide; that a trill shall accord with its definition and not be a flutter on one note, nor fall under such a blasting characterization as that of a caustic critic of our day when he described a vain attempt at this ornament as "a gargle which the singer meant for a trill." The practice of colorature song is indispensable even to a singer who does not fully master it and never intends to display it in public, for it aids the vocalist in the attainment of abilities which all the styles require, on the Emersonian principle that one must often aim above the mark to hit the mark.

Sufficient lung power to give the proper shading

and manage the emotional climaxes is of course expected. This is so obvious that nothing more need be said about it, except to warn the music lover against the abuse of the loud tone as well as of the high tone. This abuse has always been palpable and monstrous; its proper parallel is found in the ranting of a fifth rate melodramatic stage villain. A note emitted with a shriek many degrees higher than the usual compass of the throat, or a thunderous roar that shakes the chandeliers, will generally bring down the house in a tumult of applause, no matter how inappropriate it may be or how destitute of every beautiful quality. A dog will wag his tail when his ears are rubbed; an audience will howl with delight when a tenor rushes to the footlights, spreads his arms and peals out a high C like an engine whistle; — the difference of intelligence between the canine and the human at this moment is not great. The passion for the big voice and the high voice regardless of all other considerations is the enemy of every fine feeling and encourages nothing but coarseness, vulgarity, falsehood. To singers addicted to such claptrap and to music lovers who applaud it, Hamlet's advice to the players is forever pertinent.

After all is said about voice and technique (and it must be admitted that pure tones, skilfully controlled, are to be sought for with zeal unceasing), yet the higher criticism affirms that these things are tributary to expression, that singing is the rendering of words with a view to reënforcing the ideas, sentiments, and emotions set forth in the text. The music lover must not be wholly carried away by a ravishing voice and flawless execution; he must listen through the tones to the words and must insist that the singer, like the actor, shall enunciate distinctly and pronounce correctly, and that every detail of phrasing, tone color, shading, and tempo shall be guided by the one unflagging determination to make the style of the song suit the spirit and diction of the verse.

To sustain the correct sound of the vowels and the precise articulation of the consonants, and at the same time preserve the proper quality and amount of tone, is no doubt extremely difficult in many situations, and the singer is constantly under temptation to sacrifice the former to the latter. The hearer should make due allowance for these impediments in view of the fact that he is listening to music as well as to words, that the crispness of enunciation in ordinary speech is not possible in singing, with its frequent prolongation of a vowel over many notes and the special stress laid upon the musical vowels as compared with the unmusical consonants. Taking these considerations into account, the listener has the right, nevertheless, to expect that within the limits prescribed by the very nature of the vocal art the singer should remain faithful to the belief that song is one way of delivering words, and that the rightness of his work consists not only in the general conformity of style to the poetic sentiment, but also in the observance of all the refinements of vowel and consonant articulation.

It is not simply that the hearer has a right to know what the singer is singing about. Purity and truth in the mere technical utterance depend much upon verbal accuracy. "The sheet anchor of vocalists," says the eminent baritone David Ffrangcon-Davies in his stimulating book, *The Singing of the Future*, "ought to be pure pronunciation — pure in regard to linguistic fitness and arising from general culture. Pure pronunciation (musical, sustained, fitting) once achieved insures right tone production, and consequently right tone." "As good actors' tone fits the word, so also must good singers' tone fit the word. The sung word should have the penetrating power which belongs to the fine elocutionist." "Vocal efficiency depends on mental efficiency. The character of the word and not of the tone *per se* is the safeguard."

Furthermore, true artistry in song implies intellectual culture, for a careless disregard of the high claims of language indicates lack of education and of genuine delicacy of feeling. Especially must those who sing in English be heedful of this law, for the English language, with its unparalleled variety of vowel and diphthongal sounds (twenty or so may be distinguished) and its crowding of consonants, is the most difficult of the tongues to pronounce perfectly while maintaining a pure musical intonation. "Two of the greatest tests of diction," says Mr. Louis Arthur Russell, "are in sustaining correct vowel quality with all varieties of emotional color, and the ability to sustain a given emotional color throughout a phrase including a variety of consonants. This art is rarely exhibited in the English language among singers to-day." And in respect to consonants, Mr. Russell says: "The explosive element, the click or puff, the breath rush or tick of consonant making, is not musical, therefore it becomes the task of the singer and the intellectual talker to avoid all noise in consonant emission, and to give the articulating effect of these mechanical parts of words without destroying the legato flow to which the vowels lend such kindly service."

There is no more striking illustration of the ideal sought by the most advanced modern singers, both in music-drama and song, than is found in Richard Wagner's eloquent tribute to Ludwig Schnorr von Carolsfeld, whose Tannhäuser and Tristan revealed even to the composer unknown depths in his own creations. In this tribute to his lamented friend and co-worker the master makes but a single passing allusion to his "mellow, full, and brilliant voice," and of tone formation, attack, agility, and compass there is not a word. It was the artist's supreme portrayal of "the torturing conflict in Tannhäuser's soul" that stirred the composer's enthusiasm, "his frenzy of humiliation" in the second act, "the ecstasy of humiliation" in the third act; the greatness of conception and vehemence of delivery in the last act of "Tristan and Isolde," by virtue of which, in spite of the intricacy and intensity of the orchestral music, "all attention, all interest, was centred in the actor, the singer," the orchestra being "wholly effaced by the singer, or — to put it more correctly — part and parcel of his utterance."

From Rossi with his chromatic chain of trills, and Farinelli, driving the humiliated trumpeter from the field, to Ludwig Schnorr and Albert Niemann, intent only on forcing the word and the emotional situation into the consciousness of the auditor, the ideal of the vocal art has indeed made a long and devious journey. In the old days passion and psychologic interest tame and conventionalized, plot and text without independent interest, contrived only to give occasion for the display of technical skill; in the latter days the most acute emotions, elemental almost superhuman passions, projected by a Wagner or a Strauss with an energy that bewilders the mind and shakes the heart. In one case the beauty of physical sound and delicate manipulation, in the other the beauty of intellectual conception, dramatic accent, truth to the facts of the human spirit in its most urgent self-realization.

Let the noblest features in these two ideals be combined and the consummate artist, godlike among his fellows, would appear. It is not impossible. Once and again the world has seen a near approach to the longed-for paragon. Wagner at least never for a moment believed that poetic expression and refined vocalism were exclusive of one another, that there is any inherent disharmony in their natures. The principles and standards of great singing are now virtually agreed upon, and the lover of music need not go astray in his judgments. The style may alter under the varying exigencies of recitative and aria, opera singing, church singing, song singing, the *bel canto* of Handel, the declamation of Wagner,— but the universal laws of the art remain, the application of them adjusting itself to the multifarious shades of thought and feeling that give to poetic works their special form and spirit. Appropriateness of delivery to theme, to musical and poetic character, must always be the amateur's desire. Back of the tone, inspiring, directing, coloring it, is the word. If both demands — technical perfection and truth of expression — are gratified, then let the hearer rejoice — rejoice because a noble artist has come into the world, and because he is himself able to appreciate a finished achievement of art.

CHAPTER IX

THE PROBLEM OF EXPRESSION: REPRESENTATIVE MUSIC

EVERY thoughtful lover of music finds that both before and after the enjoyment of masterpieces a multitude of questions spring up in his mind, all pointing toward the one supreme, inclusive problem of art. What is the real nature of music? he will inquire. What is the ultimate motive that inspires the creations of its masters? What does it mean to *me?* What part does it play in the full life which I live in common with others? In my appreciation of it, what is the value of the technical features which I am told I ought to understand? Is the study of form, harmony, methods of performance sufficient in itself, or is it a preparation leading on to higher issues? That music is an art of expression rather than a temporary amusement for the sense seems plain to all who look beneath its surface, otherwise it never could have gained the place in human affairs which the ages have assigned it, never could have won its unshakable hold upon human affection. If music is an art of expression, what does it express? What are the scope and limits of its expressive power? What are the means that music possesses for that utterance which reaches below the sense perception, below the acquirements of the understanding, transmits a message from the soul of the composer to the soul of the listener, and establishes a sympathy between any single hearer and his neighbors in the concert hall? What may we look for when we hear music — shall we receive definite communications of thought and the awakening of the visual imagination as in poetry, or is regulated sound restricted to the stirring of a vague and intangible sense of awe or delight like that which one feels in cathedral aisles or among the parterres of artfully arranged gardens? In a word, has music a meaning? And if so, is this meaning imparted by direct action of sound or through association of ideas? These questions, and many more, come before the lover of music who wishes to derive the utmost value that the art is able to afford.

Some of these queries can never be fully answered; the attempt to discover the final secret of the power of tone upon the emotional nature leads to an insoluble mystery. The fact that this mystery is present in every musical experience is one cause of the peculiar fascination. The music lover finds, however, that his excitation by music is due at times to the direct, immediate action of sound, at other times partly or wholly to association of ideas. In the first case the word "expression" is somewhat misleading, for it necessarily carries the notion of something to be expressed, and that something other than the very essential nature of the means of expression. For example, we say that a piece of music is beautiful, not that it expresses beauty; that it is, perhaps, rapid, not that it expresses speed. To be sure, we may say that a piece expresses cheerfulness, but as a multitude of compositions, totally unlike in melody, harmony, and rhythm, may convey the same notion, the mere fact of suggesting cheerfulness adds very little to the value of the music to our minds. It might be better to apply Edmund Gurney's term "impressive" to music of indeterminate meaning, rather than expressive, for if we feel such music to be beautiful and uplifting, our enjoyment seems to be brought down to a lower plane if we justify it on the ground of a state of mind that is transient and superficial.

One discovers at the very beginning of acquaintance with music that it does not remain at the stage of vague suggestion, but has something in its veins that enables it to ally itself with ideas that inhabit a world outside of that purely abstract sphere to which it is confined so long as we think of it as composed only of artificial combinations of sounds. A great deal of music seems to us not merely impressive but expressive, and we often find our minds turned in definite directions, leading to actualities, when we seek to explain the hold it has upon us. So strong is the conviction on the part of many music lovers that no music is without some background of precise thought or feeling, that they constantly speak of fine music or fine performance as "expressive," regardless of the classifications of the æstheticians, suspecting that differences among musical works in this respect are differences of degree and not of kind, and that even the most formal and abstract type, such as a classic sonatà, fugue, or set of variations, is stealthily trying to impart something that its composer had seen or felt, and has a significance beyond that of mere tonal decoration.

In the present chapter I am concerned with the expressive power of music as distinct from its impressiveness, seeking to indicate to the music lover what he may properly look for besides mere agreeable tone patterns; striving also to assist him to form just judgments upon some of the attempts on the part of composers to win for their art a representative power, akin to that of the arts which convey exact ideas and deal with accepted symbols and concrete imagery. I shall try to remove certain misapprehensions to which many casual hearers of music are subject, showing what the composers who are identified with the various types of music really attempt to do, and suggesting the proper manner of applying those standards of appreciation by means of which the different degrees and methods of musical expression may be kept distinct in the listener's mind.

In order to clear the ground a few preliminary explanations are necessary.

The world of musical composition is divided into two main departments, viz., vocal music and instrumental music. Vocal works are themselves commonly composed of two elements, the voice part and the accompaniment. In the former the apparatus that produces the tone is not used for that purpose only, but also for the communication of definite thought. The ideas set forth by the words control the form and style of the music, and the tones, therefore, do not exist merely for giving pleasure to the ear, but also for the sake of bringing the mind of the hearer into accord with certain clearly realized conceptions. The music becomes not merely impressive, but representative or illustrative.

Instrumental works may be divided into two general classes: first, those which are concerned with the musical imagination solely, which contain no indication of any connection in the composer's mind with an experience or fancy that is derived from the external world, requiring of the hearer no knowledge of any fact, physical or metaphysical, beyond the rhythms, combinations, and tone colors of the musical piece itself. The listener may interpret such music in terms of concrete imagery if his bent of mind inclines him that way, — he may see dancing peasants in a Mozart rondo or a kneeling worshipper in a Beethoven adagio — but this is his own affair, for the composer gives him no hint that tends to turn his thought away from the contemplation of pure musical beauty. Works of this character have no precise titles,— only such labels as serve to indicate form, tempo, or general character, such as sonata, fugue, prelude, theme and variations, andante, presto, scherzo, étude, nocturne, fantaisie, reverie, caprice, and the like. Any one of these designations would apply to a large number of pieces of quite dissimilar style. Such music is called "abstract" or "absolute" music.

The other class of instrumental compositions is known as "representative," "illustrative," or "program" music. The composer puts at the head of his work a title or description which applies directly to this particular piece and could belong to no other. It associates the music at once with a definite conception that can be told in words; it arouses the image making faculty in the mind of the listener; it invites him to receive the music not as an emissary from a world of abstraction known only to the musical consciousness, but as an ally of poetic ideas, as a work whose peculiar character is drawn from an experience preliminary to it, and derives a considerable part of its value from the clearness with which it illustrates an idea that has in itself an independent interest. The composer chooses a character, scene, or story from history, myth, or poetry, or he recalls a personal observation of nature or human life, or perhaps invents a tale or picture for himself,— then calling upon his powers of musical creation he writes a work which will be molded and colored by the literary or pictorial antecedent. Sometimes, as Schumann tells us, the music, begun without any such object in view, suggests a train of thought or imagery to the composer, the mental eye, gradually awakened, holds fast to certain outlines amid the sounds, and the phrases condense and shape themselves under this new influence. Examples of this tendency could be adduced by the hundreds, — overtures to modern operas; symphonic poems, such as Liszt's "Tasso," Strauss's "Death and Glorification"; program symphonies, such as Beethoven's "Pastoral" and Raff's "Leonore"; piano "character pieces," such as Schumann's "Carnaval," Liszt's "Years of Pilgrimage," MacDowell's "Sea Pieces" and "Woodland Sketches." It is evident that here is a close analogy to vocal music. The difference is that no words are heard during the progress of the music; it is a sort of inarticulate song or drama; the subject once announced in the title or "program" retreats into the background of the listener's consciousness, only to be evoked in a shadowy way as he discovers in the tone color and rhythms a mysterious something that guides his fantasy as well as delights his ear.

In the attempt to determine the nature and the extent of the expressive power of music, we feel the need of drawing comparisons between music and the other arts, surveying her boundaries and theirs, discovering where these boundaries diverge and where they coincide or overlap. Does expression in music, we ask, signify the same as expression in poetry, or does the word involve a special and distinctive connotation of its own? In order that speech and music may combine in mutual support they must have some element in common. In order that music may appear as appropriate to text or title in song, opera, or symphonic poem it must at least be able in itself to turn our mind in a definite direction, and the current of feeling that is set in motion by the words find itself drawn by a subtle affinity to the feeling aroused by the music.

Writers on æsthetics love to separate the arts into two classes, viz., arts of presentation and arts of representation. The second category includes poetry, sculpture, and painting, — representative by reason of the fact that the subject matter with which they deal exists before the work of art comes into being, and is susceptible to an indefinite number of forms and modes of treatment. Poetry may have for its subject a state of mind or an outward event or scene. Any kind of visible object, or an imaginary object having no counterpart in nature but composed of forms that have an actual existence in other relations (such as an angel or a centaur), may be the subject of a statue or a picture. In representative art, in other words, the idea and the form are not completely identical. These arts, even poetry, have also been called arts of imitation, because they reproduce in new guises and relations that which has already been the object of observation or experience.

In the presentative arts, on the other hand, including music, architecture, and the various artistic crafts (such as pottery, metal work, wood and ivory carving, textiles, etc.) the representative or imitative element is either absent or is reduced to such subordination that the beholder is but casually reminded of anything that has been the object of a previous experience. The idea, generally speaking, is contained in the form, virtually identical with it, and has no existence separate from the artist's conception. The forms are abstract, proportional arrangements of lines, masses, colors, or tones; the beauty is in the pattern or design apart from those resemblances that would move us to demand truth to nature as a fundamental condition of approval. This statement must, of course, be qualified; a representative element often exists, there is a borrowing from nature; leaves and flowers may afford patterns for ornamental work in cornice and vase designs,—even animal and human forms may be so used; music sometimes admits imitations or at least obvious suggestions of natural sounds. But in all these cases truth to nature is subservient to a decorative purpose. A decoration may be defined as a form of artistic contrivance which has its interest in itself, apart from any object depicted or thought conveyed. Architecture, music, and the artistic crafts may be called arts of decoration, as distinct from the arts that teach or inform as well as please.

This division of the arts into presentative and representative has, however, little value besides convenience of classification; in a deeper view of the case the distinction everywhere breaks down. They are all presentative as well as representative, impressive as well as expressive, for they exist primarily not to give instruction or to reproduce nature, but to give pleasure. They offer themselves frankly to the senses; they make us glad, not because we have received an addition to our store of information, but because they have warmed and fed our emotional nature, awakened a consciousness of a purer ideal, stimulated a keener sympathy by the communication of spirit to spirit. Poetry, painting, and sculpture may indeed be employed for the purpose of conveying scientific or moral truth,— other things being equal, the higher the truth the higher the worth of the work of art. But just at the moment when this definite instructive or homiletic purpose becomes the apparent aim of the work, the appeal to the æsthetic sense becoming merely incidental, then the very element that constitutes art tends to withdraw from the work or from the receiver's consciousness. Never ought the decorative principle to be ignored. The outlines, modelling and grouping in sculpture, the arrangement of lines, colors, lights, and shadows in a painting, the rhythm, metre, and mellifluous disposition of vowels and consonants in verse — these decorative features are essential even if we refuse to agree with the advocates of art for art's sake in considering them all-sufficient. The enlightened connoisseur looks at once for sculptural qualities, pictorial qualities, or poetic qualities. Says Russell Sturgis: "What has the sculptor to say so important as this,—come and see this new combination of masses beautifully composed, made up of details beautifully modelled?" The strongest motive can never commend a picture to a discerning eye if it is not beautifully wrought in composition, drawing, tone, and harmony of tints and shades. A fine picture is always a fine pattern. A painter will make a portrait not simply for accuracy of likeness, but also for satisfaction of the art sense; he will so contrive composition, adjust pose, and arrange shades and colors that the picture will give pleasure to a connoisseur who knows not the name or station of the sitter. A landscape by Turner may not give a correct topographical representation of any place on earth. The Aphrodite of Melos is perhaps not an Aphrodite at all; but it does not matter,—nameless and with the arms that might have revealed her identity forever lost, she is no less the object of the world's unwavering homage. In all these instances there is indeed truth,—it is truth that gives them their ultimate validity; but it is not scientific truth or in the ordinary use of the word ethical truth; it is general, not particular truth, a truth that is identified with beauty and finds its warrant in the pleasure of the sense, and beyond that in the consciousness that through these beautiful forms we come into vital relations with a mystic reality that survives all change.

This same element, that stirs the emotion by immediate action of the sense without the aid of the defining power of the understanding, is found even in poetry, and must be reckoned with if one would know the secret of the spell that is woven by metric accents and the selected harmonies of words. The writer chooses his words not merely as symbols of ideas, but also for the beauty of sound and rhythmic vibration obtained by skilful adjustments of accents, metrical groups, rhymes, assonance of vowels and consonants. These musical effects, as they may properly be called, are not only employed for the sake of the charm of lilting cadence and artful modulation of sound, but they possess the expressive quality of music, the especial mood which the poet desires to arouse being in no slight degree dependent upon his use of the metrical and verbal devices which suggest various degrees of motion and force. Every poet considers carefully the need of a correspondence between the form of the verse and the thought and imagery, an ecstatic spring song requiring one kind of metre, an elegy another, a battle piece another, and so on. Many of the world's famous poems are not remarkable for originality or depth of thought, but endure by virtue of a certain haunting sweetness that is not in the imagery alone, but equally in their melody.

The element to which I allude is that which vanishes when the *Æneid* or the *Antigone* is translated into English prose; it is found in "the surge and thunder of the Odyssey," in the voluptuous swell of Swinburne or Victor Hugo; it is the dying fall that comes soothingly upon the senses in an ode of Keats. It is the quality that becomes faint even to vanishing when verse is read in silence. There is no need to say, of course, that poetry is vastly more than this, that a man may be a master of verbal music and after all have little that is worth saying. Poetry is, no doubt, less dependent than any other art upon the sensuous and formal elements, but how much sound and form have to do even with the meaning itself any one can discover if he will take any great piece of verse, say a sonnet by Milton or Wordsworth, change the order of the words, substitute synonyms, break up the rhythms into unrhythmical phrases, and then see how much even of the sense is left. Such an experiment will afford an important lesson in the primer of poetry, yes, in the primer of art.

Still less in the other arts can the spiritual message be separated from the form. There is an utterance that is not the language of speech; it is incapable even of translation into words. It is found, as we have noticed, in the artful tracing of lines, gradations, and colors in painting, setting up a sort of rhythmical movement in consciousness as the eye passes from one point to another. It is found in the proportioned masses and decorative patterns of architecture, in the lines and bosses of sculpture, in the buoyant measured evolutions of the dance, in the mellow sound of a voice, in the molding of a vase, or the opulent colors of a Persian rug. It is a communication more ancient than speech, and it is intuitively understood by all who have attained a truly self-conscious life. It is the business of the art lover to clear his senses and cultivate in himself that capacity which responds to the touch of beauty in whatever guise of shape or color or sound. The common man, being confined to language for the conveyance of his mental states, finds it difficult to realize that there are other very potent means of expression — that there are pictorial, sculptural, and musical ideas as well as verbal ideas. The appreciation of art expands as soon as one perceives that there are broad regions of spiritual experience which words cannot traverse, and that the other arts find spheres of action beyond the line where language ends. We must, therefore, study their *mode* of utterance — their technique, in a word, for "the sensuous material of each art," to employ Walter Pater's classic statement, "brings with it a special phase or quality of beauty, untranslatable into the forms of any other, an order of impressions distinct in kind. These impressions have this in common, however, that they give pleasure to the senses of sight or hearing; and this beauty is an end and not a means — adding nothing, it may be, to that experience and efficiency which the ordinary mechanical duties of the day require, but giving us consciousness of a fuller, more perfect life, in which our separate existence is for the moment merged."

It is in view of this attribute of all fine art which I have endeavored to describe that Walter Pater, in his well known essay already cited, declares that music "is the true type and measure of perfected art," because "music presents no words, no matter of sentiment or thought separable from the special form in which it is conveyed to us." All art, Pater goes on to say, is constantly laboring that the form, the mode of handling, "should become an end in itself, should penetrate every part of the matter." "Art is always striving to be independent of the mere intelligence, to become a matter of pure perception, to get rid of its responsibility to its subject or material." "It is the art of music which most completely realizes this artistic ideal, this perfect identification of form and matter. In its ideal, consummate moments, the end is not distinct from the means, the form from the matter, the subject from the expression; they inhere in and completely saturate each other; and to it, therefore, to the condition of its perfect moments, all the arts may be supposed constantly to tend and aspire. . . . Therefore, although each art has its incommunicable element, its untranslatable order of impressions, its unique mode of reaching the 'imaginative reason,' yet the arts may be represented as continually struggling after the law or principle of music, to a condition which music alone completely realizes."

That such a tendency as Pater here declares is found in *all* art may be disputed — his statement is too sweeping. That the "idea" is not separable from the special form it has taken is to a certain extent true of all art — the very definition of art is involved in this — but the fusion is more complete in some instances than in others. There are works of sculpture and painting which appeal "directly to the roots of emotion and sensation," and stir the mind in ways which words are quite unable to explain. Take, for example, Michelangelo's recumbent figures upon the Medici tombs, and consider the number of wholly unsatisfactory interpretations that have been drawn from them — unsatisfactory not because the sculptor expressed nothing in the statues, but because he expressed so much, expressed ideas so profound that language fails to encompass them. It was not affectation that impelled John Addington Symonds, in presence of these grand and mysterious shapes, to call up phrases of Beethoven. For it is only music that has the power of evoking ideas so mighty and extended as those which Michelangelo's oppressed giants so dimly body forth. Sculpture and music are the arts most adequate to render the one universal theme of all art, which is the striving of the soul for release from all that restricts its powers.

Although Pater's assertion in regard to art in general needs to be qualified and limited, his statement in regard to the nature of music, that the subject is not distinct from the expression, may be accepted. Change a note in a passage and the idea is changed, for the passage has no meaning apart from the particular note successions that compose it. Neither can music define or describe or personify. Music is sometimes called a language, but it is not a language. Words are artificial counters which have been agreed upon by all members of any nation or tribe as standing for certain objects or mental concepts. But there are no tones or groups of tones which have been adopted as symbols of particular objects of perception or thought. I may say, for instance: The white birch tree is putting forth green leaves. The verb, the nouns, and the adjectives are conventional collocations of sounds and letters applied by common consent to certain objects or processes. But there are no chords or musical phrases that have been fixed upon to convey the notion of tree, leaf, growth, whiteness, or greenness. A composer may have a budding birch tree in his mind when he writes a piece of music, and his composition will have delicacy, lightness, grace; but the listener may be reminded of a very different object, or of no object at all.

In comparing music with poetry, John Addington Symonds writes: "The sphere of music is in sensuous perception; the sphere of poetry is in intelligence. Music, dealing with pure sound, must always be vaguer in significance than poetry, which deals with words. We cannot fail to understand what words are intended to convey; we may very easily interpret in a hundred different ways the message of sound. . . . The exact value of a counter is better understood when it is a word than when it is a chord, because all that a word conveys has already become a thought, while all that musical sounds convey remains within the region of emotion which has not been intellectualized. Poetry touches emotion through the thinking faculty. If music reaches the thinking faculty at all, it is through fibres of emotion. But emotion, when it has become thought, has already lost a portion of its force, and has taken to itself a something alien to its nature. Therefore the message of music can never rightly be translated into words." Mr. Birge Harrison compares music to color in the art of painting. "Both are sensuous and passional, playing directly upon the emotions and producing their effects by some mysterious appeal to the subconscious, whose ways have as yet eluded us. Both, in their highest expression, come nearer to the perfect ideal of beauty as felt and understood by humanity than any other form of art. Finally, both are stimulating and mentally suggestive, while attempting no direct intellectual expression."

In the interest of the intelligent appreciation of music, it is important that these distinctions should be anchored in our minds lest the true beauty and meaning of music escape us. Language is definition and limitation; music by itself alone does not limit or explain; when acted upon by pure tone we are transported into a region without boundaries. For the moment that world is real, but it has not the reality of previous non-musical experience.

All this is true, and yet it is also true that composers and music lovers have not been satisfied with this vague and generalized impression which cold analysis would at first sight seem to prove is music's only province. Music has always been straining at its tether, striving to break away from its bondage and enlarge its field of action. A marked trait in music is the effort which Pater notes in passing as characteristic of all art — an endeavor to pass into the condition of some other mode of utterance and assume prerogatives that belong more strictly to the heritage of its sister arts. The art which music most persistently struggles to supplant, or else to bring into an alliance for mutual advantage, is the art of language. Hence the prevalence of "program" or "representative" music in later days, and the union of verse and tone in lyric and dramatic song from the very beginning of speech and melody.

The alliance of words and music has been constant through the greater part of human history. Abstract instrumental music, in a state so developed and specialized that it can be dignified with the title of fine art, belongs only to the last three centuries. It had its period of infancy, of gradual awakening to self-consciousness in the seventeenth century, of independent vigor and balance of faculty in the epoch of the Bachs, Haydn, and Mozart in the eighteenth century, of complete adaptability of form to the needs of expression in the masters of the nineteenth century, beginning with Beethoven. In the first two of these epochs, when independent instrumental music was passing, with many growing pains, from feebleness into full self-possession, tone wedded to words in opera, oratorio, and church music was exhibiting, under the hands of Gluck, Mozart, Handel, and Sebastian Bach, the enormous power of expression it contains when free to take its character from the suggestion of precise thought and definite situations. Taught by the success of these endeavors, composers grew more and more inclined to carry over the quality of direct characteristic expression to abstract instrumental music, in which there was to be found a freedom and variety of style that could not exist in the human voice alone on account of its physical limitations. This effort led to the rupture of the old strict instrumental forms of sonata, fugue, and rondo, as in Beethoven's last quartets and sonatas, where the instruments seem at times almost to usurp the faculty of speech. The next step (not in chronological order necessarily, but as an evolutionary stage) was program or representative music, where new forms and treatment appeared as required by conceptions to which the composer gave his hearers a clew in title, program, motto, or allusion. Every piece of representative music, therefore, is in greater or less dimensions a "song without words," a voiceless lyric, epic, or drama, claiming to employ in an independent sphere the special powers of expression which music had demonstrated while still in the leading-strings of text and stage action.

Representative music is by no means a phenomenon peculiar to the nineteenth century, but appears in many crude productions of the youthful and infantile periods. But in the nineteenth century means of emotional utterance before unsuspected have been disclosed in the natural progress from strictness to freedom in form, and in the perfection of instruments; and so far has the expressive power of tones been carried that music at times seems on the way to the invention of symbols that will come near to appropriating some of the prerogatives of language.

In this aspect of the situation the music lover finds a problem much more profound than that of training his faculties of observation in the tracing of harmonies, rhythms, and forms. This preliminary exercise in the appreciation of form is necessary, as I have tried to show, but it is only preliminary. No thinking mind will remain content with the mere admiration of skill in fashioning tone patterns of intricate device, or the mechanical dexterity of a pianist or the pyrotechnics of a colorature singer. The emotion must be aroused, and in works of human contrivance it is only emotion that can beget emotion. The composer must have felt something,—what did he feel? There is a man behind the work and he is imparting something of himself,—what is that something?

Works of musical art are not put together in accordance with mathematical formulas, — they come from life and they share the stirring unexpectedness of life. Music lovers have never been content with a pleasure that depends upon the merely decorative function of music, and music, as we have seen, is ever struggling to liberate itself from the confinement that seems inherent in its very material. Music is a mighty intensifier of emotions and moods; moreover it produces in the mind such a state of tremulous expectancy that it becomes eager to move in definite directions, just as when acted upon by words or external incitements of any kind. Liturgies, dramatic, epic, and lyric poetry have always joined hands with music because in this union there was an added strength. The most universal and powerful interests — religion, patriotism, and the love of the sexes — have always sought music as a reënforcement of their appeals. All this could hardly be true if there were no correspondence between music and the other means of expression. One would not associate together a piece of music and a bit of purely decorative work — an architectural molding or a drawing-room frieze — and imagine that the former was in any way a reflex or interpretation of the latter. We may say with confidence that there is no music that is absolutely unexpressive — a meaningless, empty play of sounds. The music may be comparatively trivial, but its effect is not that of a phenomenon wholly external to ourselves. Every positive rhythm, every rise and subsidence of tone volume, every distinctive tone color sets something in motion within us, and that something is felt as an ingrown constituent of our emotional life.

This impression is due primarily to the nature of tone as unlocalized, pervading our whole nervous organization and setting it in vibration; and secondly to our notion of music as something moving, the phrases as they succeed one another seeming to contain an idea that constantly advances until a foreseen goal is reached. The world within us and the world without us are perceived in terms of flux and change; movement is a manifestation of energy and implies to us life. Music is likewise movement, energy, and action; and when we add the emotional elements of rhythm and changes of force, speed, and color, this movement, this life, gives us the impression of proceeding from consciousness and manifesting consciousness. The musical movement may be swift or slow, now accelerated, now delayed, suggesting notions of ardency or languor, impatience or indolence, accession of vitality or loss of the same. A composition may hasten at its close into prestissimo — energy triumphant; or it may end retarded, signifying exhaustion or relief after the strain of effort. Within this movement there are incalculable varieties of rhythm, accents, interruptions, ever changing relations of longer and shorter notes, figures of innumerable modifications, all held in the control of regular beats and ordered measures — a counterpart in sound of the gestures and attitudes which make physical action so vivid an expression of feeling.

Equally abundant and positive are the expressional effects produced by the degrees of loud and soft — contrasts startling in their vehemence, shades of tone exceedingly minute and subtle in suggestion, not less efficient than changes of speed for conveying ideas of force in variation and contrast. Not less definite in significance are the changes between high notes and low notes, between consonance and dissonance. Lightness and heaviness, ease and constraint, elation and depression, sweetness and harshness, ecstasy and anguish — these and a host of other intimations may be offered in terms of differences of pitch and interval. Then there are the modifications of tone color, at times suggestive of the human voice or sounds of external nature; again imparting precise ideas by association, as the trumpet with war, the horn with the hunt and forest life, the flute and oboe with peaceful idyllic surroundings; again moving the mind to a less direct expectancy, as when the trombone peals in tones of solemn grandeur, or the bassoon or the viola diffuses around us an atmosphere oppressive with ominous voices. Take all these elements — pitch, speed, shading, consonance and dissonance, rhythm, timbre, force — try to conceive all their varieties of combination, contrast, and succession, and no speculation is able to declare the time when their possibilities of suggestion will be exhausted.

It is not strange, then, that with the hearing of music the imagination wakes from its slumber. Hardly a strain can be found in all the array of the world's music that may not be united to some reality of the soul's experience. Music is a continuous metaphor. The antithesis between abstract and characteristic beauty — between absolute and representative music — is constantly dissolving. Music contains not a mere general undefined charm of tones sensuously colored and ingeniously grouped like geometrical patterns on the wall of a Moorish mosque, but a beauty that is distinctive and determinate; not simply lifting the soul that it may subside again to the same level as before, but moving it in a particular direction and establishing it upon a new mount of vision. It is, therefore, no strained artificial connection with life that has been forced by the composers upon music; the relationship is in the nature of things, and the vocal composers and the writers of program music have sought to explore all the affinities by which music shows itself qualified in its special way to act as an exponent as well as an adornment of life.

In spite of all these considerations, there is still controversy over that form of music known as program or representative music. Although it has been accepted by a very large portion, probably the larger portion of the musical world, and is the most marked tendency of the day, there are many who deny its legitimacy and resist its progress. Few, indeed, would affirm that music is to be classed as a merely decorative art, that it has no power of expression whatever; and yet there is a type of mind that takes what one may call the mystical attitude toward music, prefers to escape from the world of actuality when listening to it, and interprets it, if at all, in the spirit of Thoreau, Browning, and Hearn, as I have quoted them in a former chapter, finding in it a refuge from the concrete, the definite, and the limited. Others wish that their fancy should not be fettered by words, title, or program, but would sketch their own pictures and dream their own dreams. The adherent of the abstract school asks with a tone of triumph if the program school has any works to show that are comparable to the titleless symphonies and quartets of Beethoven, Schubert, Schumann, Brahms, and Tchaikovsky, and the sonatas, études, ballades, scherzos, and impromptus of Chopin. The program advocate points to the revelation made by Wagner of the sublime possibilities of music when directed to definite pictorial and expressional ends, speaks of program music as yet in its infancy, and affirms that the ferment of experiment in representative concert music of to-day is prophetic of an epoch that will mark an advanced stage in musical evolution.

Wisdom decrees the grateful acceptance of the noble achievements of both schools. In the house of art there are many mansions. We can rejoice that music has now gone so far that every temperament, every opinion, may find that which is suited to its need. Our old principle comes back again to guide us, — does any single work fulfil its intention? Is it adapted to its special end? Does it satisfy the demand of one who takes his critical footing upon the composer's own ground? Is it beautiful, strong, and complete as judged by the laws that are involved in the class to which it belongs? The judgment of works of program music is not based upon the same evidence that applies to abstract music. Let us accept both, and compare individual works, not with one another, but with the standard which the purpose of each implies.

Let us now see what are the privileges and the obligations of the composer of program music, and what also must be the attitude and the preparation of the music lover who wishes to judge fairly and enjoy rightly.

It must first be observed that the presence of a specific title does not necessarily make a piece of music representative. Many works that are classed as program music are such only in name. It is well known that composers often write a piece in the abstract way, under the direction of the merely musical impulse, and then hunt about for a title that will commend the piece to the hearer's interest. A work of representative music is properly one in which the title very obviously belongs to that particular work and to no other. There must be something in the harmonies, rhythms, and tone colors that inevitably moves the mind to seek affiliations in the world outside musical forms, and the title comes in to lend assistance. The value of the preliminary subject or program to the instrumental composer is plain. It is to him what a text or plot is to the writer of a song, oratorio, or opera. His musical invention is stimulated; new forms, new harmonies, rhythms, and tone colors spring to life in his imagination under the touch of some external image or inward recollection. To the wide prevalence of this incentive is largely due the vast expansion of musical resources that is a distinguished feature of our age. It is a tendency which has emancipated music from laws which would soon have become burdensone. Strict forms relax as a new principle of cohesion is substituted. Inexhaustible variety ensues in all the appliances of musical expression, and invention rejoices in the thought that complete freedom is allowed so long as truth to the spirit of the subject is maintained. The old law of conformity to type having been abrogated, each work acquires an individuality. Music thus joins with the characteristic tendency of the nineteenth century, by which art has broken away from academic authority, permitting the artist, whether he be poet, painter, sculptor, or musician, to follow gladly the dictates of his own genius, to choose whatever subject in nature or human life seems to him worthy of presentation, and to treat it in his own personal way, not a conventional way taught in the schools, encouraging him to find beauty in character as well as in form, to break down the barrier that formerly existed between art and the larger human concerns, to make art in the broadest sense a confederate of reality. The spirit of the artist now has free play, and art, shaping itself anew, creates a new technique while it pursues a new ideal.

It is, of course, possible that music, like painting and sculpture, may go so far in this direction that ugliness results instead of beauty. Music has so little power of characterization that the loss of sensuous beauty cannot be made good by those compensations which the other arts have at their command. A picture like Watts's "Mammon," or a portrait of a court dwarf by Velasquez, where ugliness becomes a means of conveying truth, can have no precise counterpart in a musical composition. Composers, however, are showing discontent with the precept, accepted hitherto as involved in the very nature of music, that expression must not go beyond the pleasure of the ear. Something much like musical realism — if such can exist — is attempted by Richard Strauss and others of his school. Strauss affirms by implication that music may deal with what is physically or morally repulsive, and may, even logically must, become ugly in fulfilling its office of dramatic expression. It is possible that the musical world will eventually grant to music this privilege of foregoing beauty for the sake of characterization. If so, restriction will probably be applied to the choice of the subject for representation rather than to the expressive development of music itself.

How far harshness and formal license may be carried for the sake of expression is one of the absorbing æsthetic questions of the day. The determination is not quite the same in program music as in the opera. The two cases are not quite parallel. Characterization will give less displeasure in dramatic music when it runs to extremes of violence and roughness because the musical effect does not stand alone; it is only one ingredient in a compound in which words, action, and scenery take up music into themselves and subdue it to the common intent. But in a concert orchestral piece the program, once read, is put aside and fades into the background of consciousness, and the music asserts itself as unrelated sound rather than as a reflection of this or that concrete idea. It must never be forgotten that in vocal music the distinct content of thought lies in the words and not in the music. In program music the content of thought has been given us before the music began, and the music has but a feeble and indirect means of keeping that thought alive. The disadvantage of a program that consists in a long series of details, as in Berlioz's "Symphonie fantastique" and most of the symphonic poems of Richard Strauss, is either that the mind will be turned away from the music in the effort to follow the program by means of the memory or, worse still, by means of the printed description, or else in concentrating the attention upon the sounds for the sake of the enjoyment of the ear the music will often appear incoherent and pointless. One might maintain, therefore, that music which requires the accompaniment of an elaborate story for its interest is an æsthetic error. Where the effort is successful in any particular instance, the success will be due to the composer's wisdom in selecting his subject, his ability to write music that is not wholly dependent upon the poetic thought for its effect, and his skill in maintaining by means of tone the vivid impression of the emotional groundwork even after the details which supply the motive have withdrawn from the listener's mind. The difficulties indeed are great; so great that program music is still in the experimental stage.

I have spoken of the value of a program to the composer in quickening his invention and inducing variety in his forms and colors. Now what is the value of a program to the listener? It is not simply that the program makes the music intelligible. Good wine needs no bush, and the music of a master may fill our rapture to the brim through the sufficient glory of melody and harmony alone. The real value of a program, it seems to me, is that, like the words of a song or the plot of an opera, it arouses a preliminary mood, begets an expectation. The music is not required to awaken the hearer from a passive state; his mind is already active, on the alert for a beautiful thought or image, and when the music arises two pleasures have been created — the pleasure in beautiful sound, and the pleasure of the inward eye or the memory of something known and already loved. The hearer receives, perhaps, some noble thought in a vesture of fitting words, such as Lamartine's vision of life, chosen by Liszt for illustration in his symphonic poem, "The Preludes." Or it may be the woful story of Francesca and Paolo; the moving fate of the lovers of Verona; the sweet village idyl of Hermann and Dorothea; some splendid legend from the Greek myths or the Arthurian cycle; a romance of Arabian chivalry. Or the composer puts at the head of his piece a name, a hint, an allusion that brings before us some intimate scene of domestic life dear to the common heart. Or it may be some glorious aspect of nature, moonlight on still water, a stormy sea, a forest glade, summer twilight with the gathering host of stars, mountain summits where the sunrise plants its banner and winds chant their monotonous, everlasting song. Or the title may contain the mere intimation of joy or sorrow — a touch of nature that makes the whole world kin — a mood, a longing, a desire for human fellowship, a religious hope. In all these cases not only does the music offer an interest of characterization, but the listener finds his mood attuned to the touch of a two-fold beauty, and when the sounds begin they are haunted by another charm drawn from the presence of a cognate loveliness antedating the music, but now become a part of the endearing spell that is woven upon his imagination.

Accepting program music, not only as legitimate on æsthetic principles, but also as an inevitable stage in the evolution of tonal art, the music lover has only to consider the value to himself of the particular works of this class that may come to his attention. He may inquire, Is the subject worthy of the use the composer has made of it? Is it suited to the special nature of musical expression? Does the music conform to the idea? And, most of all, does it have an artistic value over and above its cleverness as illustration? Music that has no merit in itself is none the better because the composer has shown a fine poetic taste in his choice of a motive. Many inferior musical pieces, like unworthy individuals, are received into good society on the strength of reputable introductions. It is a common error in respect to vocal music,—a beautiful poem, a sublime Scripture, a strong oratorio theme or opera plot will often beguile the hearer into imputing to the music a merit which it does not possess in its own right. It is the old trap into which so many fall who are always, often unwittingly, looking for literary values in art instead of musical or pictorial or sculptural values.

Equally in error is the listener who cares only for music in the abstract, ignores the subject, judges the music as he judges an untitled sonata or string quartet, pronouncing the music good or bad as the melodies and harmonies please him or do not please him. If the title or program meant nothing in relation to the composer's inspiration he would not have chosen it, and if it meant something to the composer it means something to the hearer. One of the fundamental canons of art criticism is that the critic must take the artist's standpoint, and appraise the work in accordance with the completeness with which it fulfils its author's intention. Program music always contains features which would not be there if they had not been suggested by certain elements in the program, and the critic must interpret them with an eye to their character as illustrative material. It is the same principle that holds in vocal music, and it is contrary to reason to accept the principle in the one form of art and reject it in the other. And yet men have implicitly disowned it even in vocal music. Long struggles were needed to get it adopted in the judgment of the opera. Wagner's early opponents were in most cases people who refused to hear his music as an outgrowth of the poetry and the scene, and because they could not find in his works that particular form and quality of melody to which they had been habituated they tried their utmost to drive those superb creations into outer darkness. Judged by this false standard some of the finest modern songs would miss their aim, even if they were not declared positively offensive. If the composer has something definite to express and conveys it with telling force, then the music takes into itself some measure of the beauty or power of the poetic theme, and although one kind of value may seem to be sacrificed for another, yet if the composer is a master of his art and can penetrate the harsh or irregular music with the heart throb of a genuine emotion the hearer receives an abundant compensation.

It is the duty of the hearer, in the case of representative instrumental music, song, cantata, or opera, to possess himself of the poetic subject — the program in program music, the poem in the song, the plot and significance of the characters in the opera — as fully as possible before the work is performed; then with his mind properly adjusted in view of the composer's intention he will be in a position to do justice to the composer's achievement. Considering the vast range of suggestion which modern music covers, this obligation involves rather large acquisitions on the part of the habitué of concerts and operas. Only an encyclopedic knowledge of history and literature would enable one to meet all the works of the modern composers with a sufficiently prepared mind. In order to realize this, let one peruse such books as Mr. Lawrence Gilman's *Story of Symphonic Music*, Mr. George P. Upton's *Concert Guide*, or any of the numerous handbooks of operatic plots. Intimate acquaintance, however, is more profitable than special "cramming," and other things being equal the man of wide familiarity with the records of human thought will have an advantage over another whose literary experience is more restricted. It is obvious that one who has never read *A Midsummer Night's Dream* will miss much of the charm of Mendelssohn's overture. He will get the melodies and tone colors, but he will not get the characterization. And a conductor who puts this overture on a concert program will not print an abstract of the play — a certain amount of knowledge of Shakespeare on the part of the audience he will take for granted. A composer who draws his motive from the Hebrew Scriptures, from *The Iliad*, from *Faust*, from *The Divine Comedy*, from *The Idylls of the King*, from the Greek or Norse mythology, assumes an acquaintance on the part of the public which every music lover should wish to justify so far as he himself is concerned. His general culture should be able to meet the composer's challenge, but if it does not, let him not despise the help which the commentators offer him.

I have said that all music is in a certain sense expressive, representative. Notwithstanding, the most literally imitative piece of program music exists for something better than description or illustration, its worth, if it is worth anything, is that it transcends its theme. The æstheticians have shown us that the school of realism in painting and fiction can never fulfil its avowed intention because an exact reproduction of nature is impossible in art, and that the painter or writer must render nature as *he* sees it, and can never escape the law that every impression is modified by the nature of his temperament, his habits, and his convictions. In music realism, in the conventional sense of the theorists, does not exist at all; the most literally minded among the program composers gives us not a delineation, but an emotional reaction delivered to the listener in abstract musical terms. The musician's forms are of his own creation, having no models in nature. His materials — notes of various pitch and timbre, combined in rhythmic phrases and harmonic groups — have primarily an independent beauty of their own, and secondarily an expressive character through symbolism, analogy, and association, together with a very slight imitative quality which acts far more by suggestion than by an actual reproduction of natural sounds.

In view of this let the music lover accept the expressive gift of music, lending due weight to the real purpose of text or program and its ability to guide the imagination, and then listen with mind absorbed in the music and not intent on finding pictures or stories in every passage that strikes him as unusual. People ask, What does this or that music "mean"? What does the opening phrase of Beethoven's Fifth Symphony mean? And one imagines that something of great importance has been added when one is told that Beethoven said: "Fate knocks at the door." The trivial "interpretations" in which musicians sometimes indulge move one to something stronger than impatience. A professor of music in one of our colleges, writing in a magazine on the subject of teaching musical appreciation, advises that students be encouraged to look for descriptions in the pieces they hear. He cites a passage in Chopin's Ballade in

G minor, and says that it depicts a cavalcade of knights and ladies. Is a group of men and women on horseback very important to us? Does the glorious music of Chopin's masterpiece appeal to nothing deeper than a child's delight in a circus procession? Will this expounder of the sublime in terms of the trivial inform us which phrase describes a horse's tail, which chord is a knight's plume or a lady's head-dress? The poet Sidney Lanier, after asserting in *Music and Poetry* that "musical tones have in themselves no meaning appreciable by the human intellect," a few pages farther on, with delightful inconsistency, gives us an "interpretation" of Beethoven's Seventh symphony, in which he imagines the composer "coming back from a journey under bases of mountains and telling us what he saw," and speaks approvingly of some one's comparison of the third movement to "the flight of bats and swallows from a ruin." Is not this pathetic? Alas for him, be he poet or clown, whose mind is occupied with bats when breathed upon by that heavenly song in D major!

If those who give their lives to music are misled into degrading their musical experiences, the odd perversities of the uninstructed need not surprise us. A psychologist, who is investigating the phenomena of musical receptivity, informs me — what perhaps I should have known before — that certain literalists believe, for instance, that music may express anger, and to such an extent that one who hears it will feel indignation even to the manifestation of it in flushed cheeks and clenched fists. If such an effect could occur and were at all frequent, orchestral conductors would need to take precautions for their safety, for no one could tell when such music as that of Wagner's Alberich robbed of his gold might excite some choleric occupant of a front seat in the parquet to actual physical violence.

Let us take high ground in our musical enjoyments, and believe that in the last resort the essential things in music are so profound that only her own idiom can declare them. We may properly give the rein to our imagination, but let us not pervert the composer's message or transgress the laws of art. What music is, in its final analysis, even its masters do not know. Schumann, while explaining that musicians are often affected by outward influences and impressions, declares that "people err when they suppose that composers prepare pens and paper with the deliberate predetermination of sketching, painting, expressing this or that." "Where the youth of eighteen hears a world-famous occurrence in a musical work, a man only perceives some rustic event, while the musician probably never thought of either, but simply gave the best music that he happened to feel within him just then."

The problem of the nature and extent of musical expression is the most difficult in art. Each music lover must solve it for himself. It is beyond doubt that there are hidden meanings in multitudes of works that bear no title and are connected with no text. Tchaikovsky wrote his explanation of his fourth symphony for Madame von Meck, not for the public. We know that his impressive and baffling "Symphonie pathetique" had a program, but that is all we know. Beethoven unquestionably could have given titles in many cases where he refrained. The music of every great composer is certainly molded and colored by his conceptions of life, his joys, and his sorrows. To say that a composer keeps himself out of his music is to say that his music has no life. Chopin's "revolutionary étude" was surely not the only outburst of distress that his works contain. "My music," said Schubert, "is the outcome of my genius and my misery." Berlioz's extraordinary *Memoirs* may be read as an indirect commentary on his compositions. Wagner's "Tristan and Isolde" and Schumann's songs of the year 1840 are the outburst of emotion excited by peculiar influences belonging to a distinct epoch in their lives. And so we might go on inferring revelations in unknown instances from the many that we know. In these mysteries lies much of the peculiar fascination of music. Within just and reasonable bounds we may accept them, and use them to enlarge our sympathies while our senses rejoice in the abstract beauty of sound.

We must observe, however, that program music is not completely supplanting its sister in the household of art, as many critics seem to believe. Abstract music, so called, is not out of date, any more than music without words, as Wagner held, has accomplished all that is in it to do. A strong program tendency is indeed apparent, increasing perhaps, but as yet by no means dominant. Most of the symphonies of Tchaikovsky, Dvořák, and others of the later school, all the symphonies of Brahms, are without titles or programs. The illustrative experiment has hardly touched the vast field of chamber music. Few of the numerous piano and violin concertos have definite subjects. Moreover, it does not yet appear that the program symphony and the symphonic poem have greater achievements to show than the symphonies of Beethoven, Schubert, and Brahms, the D minor and C major symphonies of Schumann, and the Fifth of Tchaikovsky; neither has illustrative piano music surpassed the creations of Chopin, whose designations of ballade, nocturne, etc., are not titles in the sense in which the student of program music uses the term. These and other great works of the abstract school may be interpreted indeed, but in terms of our own emotional consciousness, and this perhaps will commend them more strongly to our affections than those works which, by reason of their descriptive titles, involve an interest that is partly or wholly objective. In the long run those works of art will be most cherished which emanate spontaneously from the inner spiritual life of the artist, as compared with those that are made in accordance with an influence that is purely external. The latter, however masterly in invention and design, will often bear a more or less evident stamp of artificiality. We know that Beethoven's greatest works are the expression of his own moods and spiritual struggles, and I am sure that they are more impressive on that account than if we knew that they were musical reproductions of incidents in his own life or the attempted portrayal of scenes in history or fiction.

After all it matters little, for in the last analysis music is in its essential nature universal and subjective. In its inability to describe events, in its unrivalled power to idealize, lies its glory. Let the partisans of the abstract and the program schools wrangle and exhort. Both are justified, both have their necessary place in the economy of art, and when we look below the surface we see that they have a common basis. We have only to accept the composer's evident intention as a guide to the appraisal of his work, and to measure every musical production by the artistic principles which its special nature involves. After all, the different types of art reach very much the same purpose by different ways. One great law sustains them all. "Truth," says Professor Dowden, "is the means of art; its end is the quickening of the soul."

CHAPTER X

MUSICAL HISTORY AND BIOGRAPHY

How much should the amateur know of the history of music and the lives of the composers he loves? Is it necessary that he should know anything? He does not need to be told that musical works are not solitary, that all attach themselves by a thousand invisible fibres to one another and to a world of thought and feeling from which their individual form and quality are drawn; but what signifies this to the one whom they momentarily address in theatre, church, or concert hall? Nothing, perhaps, if the beautiful is merely the agreeable, if it has done its utmost when it has given us a few passing sensations of pleasure, shutting us off from all the constant fellowships of the reason and the understanding. At the moment of hearing music we are, undoubtedly, more conscious of the isolation than of the fellowships; mental concentration, as we have seen, is the condition of full appreciation; but the music lover I have in mind would not be satisfied if this absorption in purely personal sensations, delightful and essential as they are, were all that music had to offer him. Music, like all art, has, primarily, a social value. In the first place it establishes a bond of sympathy between the individual hearer and his fellow worshippers at the shrine of art. King Ludwig of Bavaria deceived himself when he imagined that those performances of his splendid opera company which he ordered for himself alone, gave him the highest degree of satisfaction that music can afford. And in the second place, when we survey music as a historic art, the product of an evolution due to known and to unknown causes, as representative of certain world movements and as the expression of the soul life of its creators, men like unto ourselves who addressed themselves directly to us in their works, appealing for our sympathetic comprehension — then a new order of gratifications is set up in our minds, the highest and best, I am ready to believe, that art can furnish.

A work of art is not of any greater worth æsthetically because it marked a crisis in a composer's life or reflected a certain phase of culture or manners. But the fringe of associations, the human suggestions, that gather around it stir our imagination into very profitable activity as soon as our quest extends into the region they inhabit. Whatever affects the state of the mind in presence of a work of art enters, whether we are immediately aware of it or not, into our judgment of its personal worth. So far as a critic is conscious of the background, looks for the larger fact which gives to the work its existence and support and finds in it a human document, so far will it offer him a peculiar kind of interest which is unknown to him who studies it in isolation and detachment. If we can bring ourselves to believe that the value of art is a social value, then we shall use works of art as a medium of comradeship between ourselves and the soul of their creator and the soul of their time. We speak of representative music as especially characteristic of the nineteenth and twentieth centuries, but in a very real sense all great music is representative. Not only the program music of our day, which strives to assume the prerogatives of poetry and painting, but even in the classic period, when art, to borrow the words of Vernon Lee, "exists for art's own sake, when men ask it only for the beautiful, when it stands in full independence" — this classic phase is also a product of evident conditions, and it means more to us if we go outside of it and survey the social and artistic tendencies of its time. Moreover, when we say that a work of art appeals or should appeal to us completely severed from external conditions, just as it is in itself, we forget that the impression of a work of art is never simple, but always very complex. It is the result of many predispositions perpared by a multitude of personal experiences and associations. A work of art cannot make identically the same effect upon any two persons, for the receiving faculty, depending as it does upon a complex train of habits and mental activities, cannot be precisely the same in both. The emotional response is largely conditioned by the kind and degree of individual expectation. If historic, social, and personal associations cluster around a musical composition the hearer's state of expectancy is very unlike that of another in whose mind this particular kind of atmosphere is lacking. There is more satisfaction to us if there seems a revelation of life in the music; if the *man* Beethoven or the *man* Schubert speaks to us in his works; if the elegant, witty, formal, eighteenth century finds a voice in the prim old harpsichord suites and Neapolitan arias; if the fervor of German piety and the dogmatic austerity of Lutheranism are heard in the cantatas of Sebastian Bach, and the passionate cry of modern pessimism and disenchantment is echoed in the bitter strains of Tchaikovsky.

I am well aware that I have now entered upon debatable ground, and I must be very careful of my words lest my meaning be misunderstood and I seem to play fast and loose with established æsthetic principles. Such analogies as I have adduced may easily be pushed too far. That way lies the sentimental "interpretation" of music which has justly aroused the scorn of clear thinkers. Protest against it has driven certain writers to the opposite extreme. Critics of the school of Hanslick and Gurney deny that the effect of music owes anything to historic or personal associations. "There is no indirect way," says Gurney, "in which music can make good that claim to our interest and attention which only its own beauty can enforce. . . . When we turn to the actual position of music in the present day, to the actual effect of those works which have any sort of true vitality, we shall find that the extraordinary power or popularity of the art is due to the isolation of its sphere, to the very fact that its roots have their place apart in our physical and spiritual nature, and know nothing of the interest or the disturbances of intellectual, social, or political life." Similarly, although much nearer to the real point, Matthew Arnold utters a warning against the fallacy that may arise in our judgments of poetry by applying the historic estimate. "By regarding a poet's work," he says, "as a stage in [a] course of development, we may easily bring ourselves to make it of more importance as poetry than in itself it really is."

In these objections there is certainly much truth, and the study of the history of art will lead to many errors if it persuades us in any instance to substitute an archæological or social or any kind of auxiliary value for the inherent æsthetic value. Arnold, however, goes on to add to his maxim a qualification which seems to me to touch the core of the issue. "The use of this negative [that is, historic or biographic] criticism is not in itself; it is entirely in its enabling us to have a clearer sense and a deeper enjoyment of what is truly excellent. To trace the labor, the attempts, the weaknesses, the failures of a genuine classic, to acquaint oneself with his time and his life and his historical relationships, is mere dilettantism unless it has that clear sense and deeper enjoyment for its end."

The acceptance of this principle will clear away many doubts from the mind of the teacher of musical appreciation who feels that the study of the art cannot wisely be severed from its historic and social background. His business is with the intelligent application of the principle. He must certainly bear in mind that the æsthetic values are primary, that a work is no more deserving of admiration because it is a link in a chain of development, that a dull piece of music is no less unprofitable because it happens to have been produced in connection with a momentous revival of religion, that the world cares little for the joys and sorrows of a composer unless his music is in itself beautiful. But when it is beautiful the enjoyment of it seems somewhat more worthy and leaves a more permanent impress when it is reënforced by a consciousness of the human impulses from which it sprung. It is another thread that binds us to our kind. For Gurney's statement is not true that "music knows nothing of the disturbances of intellectual, social, or political life." Of political life perhaps not, but it is a very superficial view of music, particularly nineteenth century music, which sees in its phenomena no correspondence with intellectual and social changes. The time will come when some scholar, equipped with sufficient learning and philosophic acumen, will exhibit modern art and literature floating on the great tide within which the thoughts, passions, and aspirations of the race are moving, and he will not exclude music from his survey. We may concede to Gurney that these large considerations may have nothing to do with our instant enjoyment of a concert or opera when new and unfamiliar works are before us; yet when we deliberately study all the phenomena of music from every side we feel instinctively that music is something more than Hanslick's "sounding arabesques," something more even than the embodiment of fugitive emotion detached from the current of life; that in it the soul of humanity finds a voice and expresses in its own mysterious way certain vital elements that help to compose the temper of its age.

It seems to me that the statement made in a former chapter in regard to the value to the hearer of the subject or program in representative music may be extended to explain — in a very general way — the significance to the music lover of the history of his art. As in representative music the ideas and feelings that the music endeavors to express are conveyed to the hearer in advance and the mind is prepared to receive certain extra-musical impressions in addition to the pleasure of abstract sound, — so it may be said that the knowledge of historic relations in music gives an enlargement to our consciousness, and music which for the moment may seem an all-sufficient fact remains in our thought as part of a greater fact. And because the problems of the past are the problems of the emotional life of all times, the student comes to perceive that in the history of the art he loves there is to be found evidence of experiences akin to his own, and he is helped to realize that in his musical joys he is one of a vast congregation, bound to multitudes in many lands and ages by one of the most tenacious of those sympathies that evince a common nature among the races of men.

These principles are almost self-evident in the case of the more definitely expressive of the arts, such as poetry and painting. They are not self-evident in music; in fact they are so recondite, so impossible to demonstrate in detail, so difficult to formulate in words, that it is not strange that some deny their validity altogether. But music comes from so deep a source, it is so universal, it has undergone so many changes under external as well as internal conditions, that it would be simply evading a difficulty to deny that it is also in the broad sense a representative art. In applying the canons of historic interpretation to music we must only be watchful to maintain proper reserve.

Art history is the re-creation of the world around the artist. It tells us whence he drew his forms, his styles, his methods, and the special tendency of his genius in its practical activity. It helps us to explain works by showing how they came to be, the influences that stirred and molded them. The prime impulse, certainly, is the artist's genius, and that we cannot fathom. But, as Emerson said, "the greatest genius is the most indebted man." His works are largely the product of his environment, which includes his early educational influences. Chopin before the full development of the piano would not have been the Chopin we cherish now; Sebastian Bach, taken in childhood to Italy and brought up among the artistic, religious, and social conditions there prevailing, would have become—we know not what. Art history shows the influence of race, of family, of education, of external circumstances favorable and unfavorable, of patronage, of prevailing contemporary ideas. It enables us to understand the condition of public taste and the special demands which institutions, locality, etc., laid upon the composer's work. It tells us also how the artist was constrained by the degree of technical development which his art had attained, by the nature of the materials he was forced to use. Art is the expression of emotion in some medium appealing to the senses. The comprehension of any art requires a recognition of the necessities imposed by the medium,— as for example the state of the language in comparing Chaucer with Shakespeare and Tennyson, the inferior knowledge of pigments, drawing, composition, and perspective possessed by the earlier Italian painters as compared with the later.

Guided by this principle the student of music sees that he must not expect to find in Beethoven's symphonies the orchestration of Wagner, nor the harmony of Elgar and Franck in the oratorios of Handel. Thus enlightened — and here is the gist of the whole matter — he is thrown back and his attention concentrated upon the elements of power that are actually present in Handel and Beethoven. In no other art does the technical attainment of the period exert so compelling an influence upon the style as it does in music. Making the proper allowance for this, and also for the action of race, epoch, common ideals, and social conditions, the student who has developed the historic sense is able to employ the standards of judgment that are applicable to each composer and school. He learns what to look for, and especially what he has no right to look for. If historic study had no other result than this it would be more than justified, for it has seemed to me that there is no more frequent cause of non-appreciation and false judgment than this of demanding in musical works, especially those of the older masters, qualities which in the nature of the case they cannot possess. The great secret of critical justice is in the ability to measure works by the standards that are applicable to them. When this habit is formed the student is prepared to take the proper point of view. He escapes the errors that arise from faulty perspective. Getting into the artist's world the observer becomes as one of his contemporaries. He attains that prime condition of true critical judgment and rational enjoyment of art, which is — sympathy.

It must still be kept in mind that æsthetic values are distinct from historic values, and it is quite conceivable that a passion for historic investigation or textual criticism may exclude the spontaneous unreasoning delight in beautiful things, such as an impulsive school girl finds in Chopin or Grieg. I certainly am not one of those who would exchange the rapture of a Wordsworth or a Whitman in the presence of nature for that of a geologist over the unexpected discovery of glacial scratches. But still there is a point where æsthetic values and historic interests may meet and sustain one another. The question of the effect produced by a work of art is only partially a question of the work in and of itself — it is even more a question of the mental attitude of the beholder or hearer. Every mental experience is the result of all the mental experiences that have gone before; it is the latest term of a series. The immediate impression of a piece of music is certainly an æsthetic one, not scientific,— emotional, not intellectual. Nevertheless the æsthetic impression, which seems at the time so simple and immediate, is really a bewildering compound made up of a mingling of all past perceptions and appreciations and habits. The study of the history of music is one of the formative influences which unconsciously sway the receptive sensibility. It is a liberalizing process; it makes the mind hospitable to a multitude of considerations which assist the proper estimate of works of various schools. It gives the mind that flexibility which enables it to shift its ground and take a station from which the work may be seen clear of intervening prejudices. The preliminary discipline seems to lend the needed warrant to the accuracy of the æsthetic emotion; it is a partial guarantee against self-deception. For the best results of knowledge come when we are unconscious of it as a mere process of intellectual acquisition, and it has become a part of feeling. Knowledge ceases to be reflective and abstract only when it has become resolved into immediate insight and direct experience.

There is no study connected with art in which "a saving grace of common sense" is more required than the history of music. When the culture of an amateur is involved, and not the research of a special investigator, it seems plain that only those fields of history need to be considered that bear some relation to his own situation and needs as an amateur. And yet even here an enthusiastic music lover will wish to avoid a too narrow restriction. The breadth of vision that comes from wide excursions will affect, although indirectly, every musical experience. Nevertheless certain schools and periods are far more important to him than others. The music lover is not called upon to exchange æsthetic pleasure for the entertainment of curiosity and speculation. I am ready to agree with Mr. W. C. Brownell that to a man thoroughly alive his own period is more important than any other. But this does not mean that works produced in his own period are necessarily and always more serviceable to him than those of the past. It is not a matter of date but of actual living power. The "Well-tempered Clavichord" is more to us of the twentieth century than, let us say, the piano works of Brahms. It is not that the "Well-tempered Clavichord" was a great work for its time, but that it is a great work now. In the productions of the older time there is more reserve, less lavishness in color, less agitation of surface than in those of the late romantic epoch, but in their reflection of the moods which are the inheritance of all the generations they have no date, but are contemporary with the latest expression of genuine human emotion. The old boundary lines which were made artificially to separate successive periods from one another have been removed; the men of old time are our ancestors not merely in the flesh, but also in mental and moral habit; while modes of expression change, fundamental feelings which issue in literary and artistic forms remain essentially the same. The difference is one of varying emphasis upon this or that phase of experience, this or that view of the universe with the resulting reactions, also a difference in the means available for expression,—but there is no emotional state, no consequent mode of utterance from the rudest to the most refined that cannot be accepted, either in reality or imaginatively, as our own. We are in touch at every moment with the heart of all mankind. In the words of the ancient poet, nothing that is really human is foreign to us. Every artist and thinker who had a sincere message for his own age has also a message for the present and the future.

If a student of the history of music enjoys the services of a teacher a word of admonition to that teacher may not be out of place. He must have convictions and preferences; — if he is not extremely wise and honest he will mistake prejudices for convictions and magnify his predilections into general laws. There is safety in placing one's chief reliance on works and composers that have survived the storms of controversy and stand before the world's regard in the calmness of assured victory. There is no essential difference of opinion among intelligent people in respect to the organ and clavier works of Sebastian Bach, the symphonies of Beethoven, the songs of Schubert, and the piano works of Chopin. Many other composers are eminent for specific unmistakable qualities, and there is no difficulty in distinguishing the salient beauties of recognized masterpieces. In cases where there are honest differences of opinion among equally competent authorities the teacher should be liberal enough to refrain from attempting to enforce his own views and disparaging the opposite. He may, for example, greatly admire Mendelssohn, at the same time being willing to admit that many good judges deny to Mendelssohn a place in the first rank of composers. The teacher's only honest course in such a case is to give the reasons for praise and dispraise that are advanced from both sides, and help his pupils to weigh opinions in the face of representative works and to form conclusions for themselves. I do not need to enlarge upon the value of this discipline in the formation of character. For character is rather to be chosen than much learning, and a flexible, catholic, wide open mind is the best result of the study of the history of music or any other study.

Besides the temptation to dogmatic assertion there is another danger into which the freedom and irresponsibility of a lecturer's position are prone to lead him, and that is the natural tendency to lay undue emphasis upon subjects in which he himself is especially interested. He may be engaged in researches in some abstruse department of history, such as mediæval notation or the development of musical instruments. He may have some favorite composer upon whom he loves to dilate. His temperament may incline him to linger in some single attractive field, such as church music or the folk song. It is hard for him to restrain his enthusiasm before his class, and he will need to check his inclination to place his own sympathies above his pupils' needs. It is proper enough that a teacher of art should have his hobbies, but he must learn to curb them in the lecture room. He must never lose sight of proportions; he must not forget that the functions of the special investigator and those of a lecturer to ingenuous seekers after truth are distinct. The safeguard is in a broad and systematized plan, calculated in advance and maintained with unflinching determination, for the teacher who simply follows the lure of each day's suggestion will often find at the end that he has wasted time in agreeable side excursions, while the view of the subject which his class has acquired remains fragmentary, disproportioned, and obscure.

In the critical study of art there are three groups of materials, viz., the actual works of art, contemporary records bearing upon them and the conditions that produced them, and the commentaries of critical scholars. The first-hand scrutiny of musical compositions is the alpha and the omega of the student's task. It should be the effort of every teacher of musical history to bring before his pupils as many of the representative works of the masters as possible, and to set them to studying these works on both the structural and the expressional sides. This seems as commonplace a remark as any lover of platitudes could desire; but it is by no means superfluous, for I have found, after long and sometimes irritating experience, that the majority of students are more inclined to read *about* works of musical art in histories and critical essays than to make direct attack upon the works themselves. The reason for this, I think, is partly indolence, partly a modest distrust of their own critical judgment when it comes to giving definite reasons. It is one of the many aspects of that trait in human nature which prefers submission to authority in place of the independent exercise of the reason. Here is, perhaps, the noblest opportunity of the teacher in helping his pupils to acquire the investigating spirit and to gain confidence in their own conclusions.

There are, of course, many periods and schools

whose production it is not possible for the pupil personally to examine. The seventeenth century, for instance, will always be more or less of a *terra incognita*, which the average student can see only through the eyes of men like Sir Hubert Parry who have boldly explored its devious ways. Few of the vast multitudes of the church compositions of the fifteenth and sixteenth centuries are accessible. Even in the case of the available works of the nineteenth century composers, the money cost, especially of operas and orchestral scores, is a formidable obstacle. In respect to the majority of works and schools, teachers and pupils alike must depend upon the reports of special investigators. And even in the cases of composers whose productions can be known to the student at first hand, he must not go to the extreme of personal independence and neglect the commentaries that have been written by men of learning and discernment. These commentaries will not merely give information, they will suggest and stimulate, they will prevent or correct false interpretations and narrow views. It follows that the instructor must know what are the best books in the various departments of his subject, he must be able to perceive the difference between a philosophic treatment of a theme and one that is scrappy and superficial. He must know how to make allowance for the personal equation and estimate the critic's competence in view of his temperament, education, and æsthetic principles. With all due recognition of the usefulness of books, the teacher must, however, keep his pupils as far as possible face to face with actual living works. He must encourage them to inquire and explore so far as their means extend, employing the opinions of others only as provocation and guidance in the formation of their own. For this point must ever be made emphatic,—the study of the history of music is not merely for the purpose of accumulating facts, but far more for discovering the meaning and uses of facts and training the critical faculty. And the desired end is found not in the instant results alone, but in the acquisition of a correct method, the preparation of the ground for study and achievement in the future. No matter how short a distance the teacher may have gone in his own original research, he must know what are the accepted methods of historical investigation, so that by and by his pupils may be able to get along without him. This should always be the teacher's aim,—to show his pupils how to walk safely when they are obliged to walk alone.

A host of questions will arise to tax the teacher's wisdom, but the art of arts in lecturing, as in reading, is that of skipping. There is no more danger of over-scantiness than there is of over-fulness. The teacher who is loaded with his subject will often revel in details, forgetting the wise saying of Voltaire that the secret of being a bore is to tell everything. In economy of material, in selection, adjustment, and balance, so that nothing essential is omitted and nothing superfluous introduced, the teacher may himself exhibit some of the shining qualities of an artist. He will do well to contrive his own scheme and not indolently adopt that of another. He may think best to study with his class the chief composers in chronological order. In that case he will state in terse form the distinguishing traits of each master, with the illustration of a few works in which these traits are especially apparent. He may, however, prefer to trace the development of the principal forms, such as the symphony, opera, song, piano music, church music. Whatever the system, the larger attention should be given to the forms and composers that touch most closely the pupil's life and needs. In American schools, for example, the history of piano music, the song, orchestral music, church music, and the oratorio should have much more time than the history of the opera. This does not mean that the opera should be neglected, for since an important motive of a history course is the preparation for the musical experiences of the student's future, the whole theory of the opera should be considered, and a general acquaintance formed with the subjects and salient characteristics of those lyric dramas that have gained a secure place in the world's regard. But in the wisest division of time that which is most representative at the present day should have preference over that which has merely a historic or local interest.

Those who have a decided leaning toward any single department of musical art will naturally wish to become familiar with the history of their specialty, and this preference may well be encouraged. The pianist should be at home in the annals of his instrument and its music, the singer familiar with the history of the song, the organist and choir leader with the ideal and development of church music and its relation to the various modes of religious worship. Yet no phase of music can be isolated; for of all the separate departments of musical art is it true, as Emerson sings of the factors in human society:

> "All are needed by each one;
> Nothing is fair or good alone."

To rise to the highest view of our theme, neither does the whole history of music stand alone. Music can never be separated from the larger life of the world. The fascination of the study of its history lies in its relation to the whole course of civilization, for although it is, so far as definite expression is concerned, the most remote of the arts from the ordinary phenomenal life, it is at the same time, as Lotze declares, the most social of the arts, and its constant striving after new forms and adaptations is the reflection of tendencies in society which reveal themselves also in arts, philosophies, manners, and institutions. Nothing is more observable in the recent progress of music than its intimate connection with literature, as shown in the opera, cantata, and program music of the nineteenth century. The different styles of church music are the outgrowth of necessities in the creeds, traditions, disciplines, and ceremonies of the great ecclesiastical orders. The national movements in those countries which have but recently entered the current of musical progress, such as Russia, Bohemia, Norway, and Finland, are to be interpreted only as we refer them back to still deeper stirrings of the popular self-consciousness. To sound these depths of musical suggestion would require an abundance of knowledge and a capacity for philosophic generalization that can hardly be expected of a musical scholar. It is enough to say that these relationships exist, and that the recognition of them, even afar off, is a mighty kindler of enthusiasm. No breadth of culture, no acquaintance with languages, literature, art, and history is superfluous to the one who wishes to solve the meaning of music and interpret its message to the ages. A lifetime is far too short to compass the circuit of its relations. The magnitude and difficulty of such studies should be to every student not a discouragement but an inspiration.

In studying the history of music we learn to emerge our scanty personal experience in the experience of the race. We acquire the open mind, the liberal judgment. We forsake prejudices and observe art works in their universal aspects. Critics of the scientific order tell us that we must repress personal predilections and apply to works of art standards that are established by the consent of the best minds. This is practicable only so far as we are able to make the judgments of the best minds sincerely our own because our reason assents to them, for an opinion accepted merely on the authority of a name can never coerce us much after we have forgotten its terms. Every estimate, to be worth anything, must be a personal estimate. It follows, therefore, that it is our duty to make this estimate comprehensive and just, so far as it lies in our power. In this adjustment of the receiving mind to the work in hand we accept the aid of history,— not only the history of forms and productions, but also the history of taste. In the sifting process of public opinion we find the only really trustworthy test of artistic value, for by this we discover whether a work has in itself a correspondence with genuine human need. Great works appear greater and small works appear smaller when brought before the tribunal of history.

Deference to the verdicts of history, however, does not annul the student's right of private judgment. "The salt of all æsthetic inquiry," says Walter Pater, "is what, precisely what, is this to *me*." It makes a vast difference, however, what there is in this *me*, what faculty of response to that which is strongest and finest and most human in art. There is little value in any culture of the intellect that is kept apart from sympathetic contact with the great heart of the world. When the mind has become expanded by the entrance of the large human sympathies, the reactions in the face of particular works and groups of works will be different from those that are felt when there is no consciousness of art's permanent social relations. Through the sympathetic action of his art the student is able to enter into the spiritual life of his fellow-men, and to feel that he is at one with them in some of the nobler interests of the soul. The ultimate purpose of the study of the history of music is to increase musical appreciation in the deeper sense of the term, to enrich the inner life by making it receptive to all those quickening influences which music in its evolution through the centuries has gained the power to exert.

Besides the historic background which imparts the social interest to groups of works and schools of composition, there is often to be found a closer and more intimate revelation where a work possesses a quality which can plainly be interpreted as a communication of the composer's self — his temperament, experience, and attitude toward life. Through a vast amount of music, especially that of the nineteenth and twentieth centuries, runs what may be called a lyric quality,— behind the work we discover the man. Not the man merely as musician, as master of musical science, or inventor of themes and forms, but the man like ourselves, who might have expressed himself in literary terms if his talent had led him that way. These personal deliverances cannot be directly demonstrated to be such; the composer is no doubt often unconscious that he is uncovering his heart; yet the message seems plainly lurking in the depths of his tones. As the yearning, tormented soul of Michelangelo is unveiled in the grandiose forms, the speaking countenances, and the strained attitudes of the sublime figures in the Medici chapel and the prophets and sibyls of the Sistine, just as the insatiable curiosity concerning life and the sympathetic love for all mankind are seen in the portraits and religious pictures of Rembrandt, so in the masterpieces of modern music a human heart may be found beating amid their melodies and harmonies, and we greet not merely the clever fabricator of tone structures but a living, striving, suffering companion. I am quite sure that, in the last analysis, this recognition of fellowship with great characters is the deepest source of pleasure, as it is the most salutary result, in the study of art. The intense desire that every lover of music has to know more about the great composers as men, through their biographies, letters, conversations, anecdotes, and the testimony of their acquaintances, is associated with a belief that their music contains more or less of the elements of a confession.

We find, to be sure, a school of artists and critics who repudiate any concern with the subjective element in literary, plastic, or musical works. The author may be morally good or bad, they maintain, optimist or pessimist or anything you please, it is of no consequence; it is the work and our psychical reactions that are important to us, not the author.

Flaubert, proclaiming the most extreme principles of realism, exclaimed: "The man [that is, the author] is nothing, th woık is everything," and apparently convinced himself that in his own novels nothing of himself is to be found. "But is it possible," asks Bourget, "that a work can possess an existence in itself and different from the mind that produced it? Does not a creation of an artist — picture or statue, poem or romance, piece of music or of architecture — have for its first condition that of being the transparence of a sensibility, the revelation, direct or symbolic, of a certain soul?" It is unquestionable that the composer conceals himself in his music far more completely than the lyric poet is able to do, but even his art is not a complete disguise — there will be something in his melodies and harmonies that betrays him. Is not the soul of the music really the soul of the man? Does it not help us in studying Beethoven to know something of him as he knew himself? Do we not find in many of his letters an almost painful effort to impart something which comes to fuller utterance in his music? Are we not more powerfully affected by that music, are we not more likely to feel human sympathy as well as æsthetic pleasure, if we have learned something of the composer's joys and sorrows, his spiritual struggles and victories? Would his music make the same appeal to our descendants as it does to us if every record of his life were to be blotted out, if they could know nothing of his personal traits or the conditions under which his works were produced, the affliction of his deafness and his beloved nephew's ingratitude, his solitude, his friendships, his proud independence, his boisterous humor, his unsteady temper, the strange mingling of coarse manners with tenderness as sweet as that of a woman, his vague religious yearnings, his love of nature, his democratic principles, his lofty ideals, his passionate devotion to his art, his unwearied quest of perfection? Sir George Grove raises the question if a certain superficiality in Mendelssohn's work may not be due to his unfailing good fortune and habitual high spirits. Was Schubert correct in saying that his best music was the product of his misery as well as of his genius? The question of the precise nature of the relation between a composer's music and his life and character is a baffling one, and an eagerness to look everywhere for exact correspondences leads to that sentimentalism which, as in the study of the history of music, we must carefully avoid. In a multitude of instances such direct connection cannot be discovered — as for e ample between Beethoven's joyous Second Symphony and the doleful "will" of about the same date, — yet it is certain that a man's outward acts and displays of temperament proceed from inner causes that are just as mysterious to us as the act of artistic creation, and to say that there is no relation between the emotional life as shown in works of beauty and the emotional life as shown in those outward signs by which men interpret the inner life, would be to assert that music stands isolated from the other arts, falsely called its sisters, and is merely a formal play of pleasant sounds, as superficial, as meaningless as its detractors have ever maintained.

While we must be on our guard against carrying our curiosity concerning a musician's life into irrelevant gossip, we are more than justified when we seek to draw from the records everything that may help us to understand the man as he really was. The most illuminating aids to this sympathetic comprehension will be found in the letters of composers, especially in the correspondence of men like Schumann, Wagner, Liszt, and Tchaikovsky, who had both a love of introspection and a gift of literary expression. Nothing is more striking in the annals of recent music than the intense desire on the part of these representative musicians, and of many others in less degree, to expose to friendly scrutiny their most cherished convictions and desires. To the art critic these documents are indispensable, for they abound in the most instructive discussions upon practical and theoretical musical questions, besides throwing light upon the author's own intentions in his creative work. In some of these writings artistic affairs are uppermost, in others personal, domestic, or social concerns predominate. In Wagner's letters both the artist and the man in every conceivable relation are revealed with an unexampled abundance and minuteness. As volume after volume of his letters issues from the press we almost wonder how he found time for any other occupation. But these letters and his theoretical books and pamphlets are to a large extent explanatory of his dramas — and these dramas, as he distinctly tells us, are always the embodiment of his opinions and his longings, the one passion of his life not being fame or wealth but to be understood. The fascinating enigma of Tchaikovsky's character almost ceases to be an enigma as we read his letters to Madame von Meck; a very essential element in the biography of this perturbed spirit is to be seen, for example, in his explanation to her of the meaning of his Fourth symphony. No one can mistake the direct relationship between the letters of these musicians I have mentioned and their compositions; their tastes, aims, and temperaments are found in both modes of expression. In Tchaikovsky's Fourth and Sixth symphonies we recognize the same swift alternation of moods, the brooding melancholy, the fierce revolt, the weakness of will, the unstable compound that results from the mingling of ungoverned impulse (so common in the Slav) with western culture that we observe in the records of his life. Liszt's joyous *bonhomie*, cosmopolitan sympathies, overflowing vitality, and exuberant enjoyment of whatever is romantic, picturesque, and splendid are evident in his compositions and in his delightful *Travel Letters of a Bachelor of Music*. No less do Schumann's taste for the more inward and sentimental phases of literary romanticism and his love of simple domestic pleasures find expression in his correspondence, his essays, his piano pieces, and his songs.

This intimate relation between art and personal life, and this propensity to supplement musical production with definite explanations, is becoming more and more characteristic of the present age. The offices of composer and expounder are frequently united; the world wants the composer's opinions of his own work and of the work of others; the musician has become a man of affairs, and his relation to the public is far more direct and intimate than of old. He comes more than half way to meet his patrons, and takes every pains to be understood by them. The composer of the nineteenth century is not only nearer to us in time than his forerunner of the eighteenth, but he is nearer in the eager approach of his heart, in his almost pathetic appeal for comprehension. In this self-revelatory character of his work he is as strictly a child of his age as the contemporary painter, poet, or romancer. The period of abstraction in music was past when Beethoven employed the standard forms as channels through which he poured the burning stream of his own passionate self-consciousness. Music has ever since, in spite of partial reversions in such men as Mendelssohn and Brahms, been intensely individual, a cry of the man as well as of the age. It is music with a purpose. The public is well aware of this, it loves more and more to discover personality in art creations, and hence the demand for musical biographies, reminiscences, diaries, and letters expands from day to day. In this attraction to the spiritual adventures of its heroes the public seems to confirm the assertion of Richard Wagner that "the severance of the artist from the man is as brainless an attempt as the divorce of soul from body"; and that "never was an artist loved nor his art comprehended unless he was also loved — at least unwittingly — as man, and with his art his life was also understood."

There is little danger, I think, that the music lover will fail to make the necessary discriminations in this department of musical interpretation. Not in every composer, by any means, do we find this direct and self-revealing individualism. Among artists we find two classes, viz., the subjective and the objective. In poetry, Goethe, who tells us that all his poems were occasional poems called forth by real circumstances, that all he published were "fragments of a long confession," is the type of the subjective artist; Schiller, who went outside of himself for his material and built up his pieces in deliberate workman-like fashion, with cool, systematic regard to proper form and technique, is the type of the objective artist. The same antithesis we find in painting between Da Vinci or Rembrandt and Raphael. Wagner is preëminently an example of the subjective musician; his dramas are as much a part of the author's self as are the poems of Shelley and Byron. The eighteenth century opera composers before Mozart and Gluck are purely objective; their works were produced to order and according to contract, their subjects were wholly conventional, their music constructed in accordance with rule and tradition. The personal interest in their work is nil, and nothing that we know of their history or character is of any value to us in the appreciation of their work. This is almost enough in itself to account for the oblivion into which these operas have fallen. Opera, like the spoken drama, is indeed essentially an objective art, for the author's purpose is to reflect nature as he sees it around him, not as it is in his own inner brooding. Nevertheless the modern opera, like the spoken play, is becoming more subjective, and the Strausses and the Debussys of our time are no more anxious than our Ibsens and Maeterlincks to keep themselves altogether out of their work.

With the composers of abstract instrumental music the problem is not so easy. It is more a matter of intuition than direct perception when we find the man behind the music. Nevertheless nothing can be more plain than that such men as Schumann, Grieg, Tchaikovsky, Dvořák, and MacDowell, perhaps, indeed, most of the leaders of nineteenth century music, wrote not because they chose, but because they must, that they had that within them which forced its way out, a burden upon their souls that gave them no peace until it was discharged. They were not journeymen under employ, like so many musicians of the preceding centuries, but free independent spirits who spoke not to order, or in conformity, but as their own separate irrepressible genius bade them speak. The statement of Wagner, quoted above, must not be taken to apply to all composers but only to those of the self-conscious order to which he himself belonged; but the application can be made to the greater number of the masters whom we most love, and it will be found, I think, that the music that touches us most deeply and which we retain in our memories is the music in which the lyric element is most apparent.

One practical suggestion is necessary here. In employing this somewhat hazardous method of interpretation which I have advised, the student must take note of the stage in a composer's development to which any given composition belongs. Every composer of note has to pass through a season of formalism, when he is learning how to use his tools, getting together the material for self-expression. In this early period he will be more or less under bondage to his predecessors, and in absorbing their work he will, in spite of himself, model his own production after their manner. There is nothing of the mature Wagner in "Rienzi"; there is much of the contemporary Vienna school in the first trios and sonatas of Beethoven; there is little individuality in the early symphonies of Schubert; Verdi did not find himself until he was past fifty. Marked originality sometimes appears almost at the outset, as in Schubert's songs and Schumann's piano pieces, but even with these composers the law will be found to hold good in other forms which they cultivated. Wagner, in his *Communication to*

My Friends, makes the very profound observation that every artist of real importance is made what he is under the direction of two orders of impressions, viz., artistic impressions (meaning thereby his lessons from the technical study of his art and the influence of other composers) and impressions of life. The student of music who wishes to get to the heart of the works of his favorite masters will take both these orders of impressions into account. In the first period of a composer's life the artistic impressions will usually be the strongest, but as he grows older he will come more and more under the sway of spiritual forces and they will gradually give a more personal color to his work.

It follows from what has been said that in studying and teaching the history of music, biography must not be kept apart from the development of form and technique. Better too much of it than too little. Keep the personal human element in the foreground. The understanding of every composer's work involves the question of how it came to be, and we must go wide and deep in our search for causes.

CHAPTER XI

THE MUSIC LOVER AND THE HIGHER LAW

The good of all ages who have been imbued with a passion for righteousness, have never hesitated to spend themselves generously for the cause they loved, the advancement of goodness; nor should those who care for what is beautiful ever hesitate to give themselves as liberally to make beauty prevail in the world.—BLISS CARMAN, *The Poetry of Life.*

IN the foregoing pages I have endeavored to show the amateur, who begins with no knowledge of musical theory, some of the principles of musical design and expression. I have tried to correct the common opinion that nothing is needed in the culture of the listener except frequent association with beautiful works and the frank surrender to immediate impressions. I trust also that I have succeeded in demonstrating that a knowledge that will immensely increase the permanent benefits to be derived from music can be obtained by any one who is ignorant of musical science, by following methods which are applied, *mutatis mutandis*, to the study of the arts of design.

There still remains a doubt in the minds of many earnest people, who will refuse to entertain the claims of art unless they can see that it makes a positive contribution to moral and intellectual progress. What has it to do with conduct? they will ask. How does it help one to meet the practical issues of every day? Does it give steadfastness to one's higher purposes? Are the hours which its votaries dedicate to it a preparation for faithful service in the world, or are they an indulgence which tends to weaken the will and promote a selfish indifference to the prosaic commonplace interests upon which, nevertheless, the health of the community depends? Is not the passion for art, when given free scope, mentally and morally injurious, or at best ethically neutral, because it tempts one by visions of exquisite delight away from the active duties and the larger sympathies?

These questions, which are constantly raised an respect to art and to æsthetic culture, seem at first sight to apply more directly to music than to the representative arts and literature. The latter are more closely connected with constant life and with mental and moral ideas. They bring life and its permanent activities directly before us. We cannot resist the thought that they are designed to instruct as well as to give pleasure, to bring the consciousness into contact with physical or mental energies as well as to make the sensibilities more delicate. They unite the world of outer experience directly with the inner world of emotion. A large acquaintance with life, therefore, seems necessary for their full appreciation.

Music, on the other hand, remains enclosed in

a palace of its own creation, which seems almost like a prison so excluded is it from the world of change and conflict. It is in the world, but apparently not of it. It seems at times little more than a fair illusion; to us, as to Jean Paul Richter, it tells of that which we have not seen and shall not see. When Matthew Arnold proclaims his famous dictum that poetry is at bottom a criticism of life — the application of ideas to life — even if we refuse to accept it as a complete statement, we confess that it contains a large measure of truth. If he had also applied the same test to painting and sculpture we should not reject it utterly. But no one, I think, would assert that music is a criticism of life — the application of ideas to life. Arnold's further claim that "the substance and matter of the best poetry acquire their special character from possessing, in an eminent degree, truth and seriousness," would again not be wholly inapplicable to the other representative arts, but could hardly be made for music. Seriousness, yes; but to speak of truth in connection with music would be to use a term without meaning unless we apply to music Keats's declaration, questionable elsewhere, that "beauty is truth, truth beauty." It is, therefore, hardly a cause for surprise that philosophers and moralists often look with suspicion upon the fascinations of music, and would restrict musical indulgence on intellectual and ethical grounds, or else would insist that some practical counter interest should be at hand to neutralize the spell which the enticing goddess of sound throws over her adorers. William James has thus solemnly spoken from his professorial pulpit: "The habit of excessive indulgence in music, for those who are neither performers themselves nor musically gifted enough to take it in a purely intellectual way, has probably a relaxing effect upon the character. One becomes filled with emotions which habitually pass without prompting to any deed, and so the inertly sentimental condition is kept up. The remedy would be never to suffer one's self to have an emotion at a concert without expressing it afterward in some active way. Let the expression be the least thing in the world — speaking genially to one's aunt, or giving up one's seat in a street car, if nothing more heroic offers — but let it not fail to take place."

Professor Vida Scudder assumes a still more austere mien as she brings this sweeping charge: "There is a class to whom the stimulus offered by music is on the whole a demoralizing influence. In their quiet and well ordered existence, where the sensational must be found not in external events, but in subjective experience, the thirst for a subtle form of emotional excitement becomes the dominant motive of life. If the end of life be purposeful activity and the function of emotion be simply to stimulate to action — then it must be seen that among the influences to which the oversensitive nature can subject itself there is none more dangerous and pernicious than music. For, more than any other power on earth, music arouses emotion without furnishing any hint of an end to which the emotion shall be directed."

This would be a formidable indictment if its premises and its implications in regard to the nature and consequences of the musical experience could be wholly accepted. As a general principle it is undoubtedly true that the end of life is purposeful activity, but surely this does not mean that we should be in a condition of physical or mental restlessness every hour of our waking existence. As it is the duty of some to think in solitude while others perform in the great world's eye, so there is a time in each man's life for escape from the duties that grind and wear, and from the emotions that know no peace until they have gone forth in action. There is a place for contemplation, for the refreshment that follows a visitation of heavenly beauty, for the inward happiness which may indeed strengthen us for purposeful activity when the proper time for it comes, but which our instinct tells us is a worthy and wholesome thing in itself, regardless of ulterior aims. In poetry, in art, in music there is, in Bliss Carman's words, "a power that stills our superficial, unnecessary self and allows our wiser, deeper self a moment or an hour of freedom." James implies that the first duty after a musical experience is to forget it as soon as possible, implicitly denying that one carries away from the concert hall anything that can profitably be relived in memory and become a restorer of the jaded spirit for the next day's toil. Music is an expression of life, and the works of the great composers are the projection of the spirit of men who thought deeply, wrought heroically, and imparted to their music the strength they won from conflict with the baffling mysteries and the stern oppositions of the world. "To quicken our life into a higher consciousness through the feelings is the function of art," said Professor Dowden, and every one who takes music seriously and has come to understand its breadth and height would indignantly combat an assertion that music does not possess this quickening power. "The emotions which I experience while hearing music," says John Addington Symonds in his *Diary*, "in beautiful scenery, before fine pictures, in cathedrals, at the thought of noble men — these enable me to understand and to enjoy, intensify the glow of life, and raise me to a higher sphere." Any one who feels in himself this consequence of great music need not distress his soul with fears that his active energy will thereby be undermined.

It must nevertheless be confessed that there is a side of æsthetic indulgence in which peril lurks, and no honest lover of art will refuse to face the dilemma. On this subject a few things may perhaps profitably be said. In the first place these perils are not confined to music, and there is a rank injustice in singling her out as a more dangerous seducer than her sisters. Certain writers are fond of asserting the superiority of poetry, painting, and sculpture to music because, as one of them declares, "they give us ideas to apprehend as well as beauty to enjoy." There is nothing more profitless than discussions over the superiority or inferiority of one art to another, but it may be asked, what is it for which the world has always adored art — its "ideas" or its beauty? The harm that the art enthusiast may incur is in a too passionate love of the sensuous, in detaching a special beauty from its proper relation to life, and in so concentrating his gaze on a superficial fascination as to permit it to hypnotize him and paralyze his will. It is a matter of record that this evil is as often found in a devotion to poetry and the arts of design as to music, and the fact that they are more directly connected with actual life does not make their enchantments any less malign. I am not alluding to their ability to corrupt by actual representation, but rather to the tendency of the art voluptuary to yield to that subtle, deceiving form of self-indulgence which exhausts his sympathy with the toils and sorrows of his fellow men while he imagines he is cultivating the finest capacities of his nature. D'Annunzio, in his novel, *Il Piacere*, has vividly portrayed in Andrea Spirelli a nature whose moral decadence had been accelerated by his surrender to the utmost allurements of the senses. "Urbanity, atticism, love of all delicacies, predilection for singular studies, æsthetic curiosity, refined gallantry were hereditary qualities in the house of Spirelli." Following his father's maxim that "one must make one's own life as one makes a work of art," Andrea had adopted as his one aim in life the ambition to develop his sensitiveness to impressions at every cost. Penetrated, impregnated with art, thirsty for pleasure, tortured by an ideal, by nature and education abhorring pain, he was vulnerable everywhere. "In the tumult of contradictory inclinations he had lost all volition and all morality. The will, in abdicating, had yielded her sceptre to the instincts, and the æsthetic sense was substituted for the moral sense." Eventually corruption did in him its perfect work.

Andrea Spirelli is by no means an isolated phenomenon in modern literature. In fact romancers of recent times, especially the French, seem to take an almost morbid pleasure in depicting the causes, progress, and results of those spiritual maladies that arise from over-indulgence in delicate specialized sensations. And it is not in fiction alone that we meet examples of moral decline accompanied by the most exquisite æsthetic sensibility. The lives of such men as Alfred de Musset, Paul Verlaine, and Ernest Dowson illustrate the dire possibilities that attend the cult of that form of beauty whose sacraments are not consecrated by virtue and administered in holy fear. There are also more robust spirits than those I have named, men and women whose ideals of art have been lofty and whose labors have been of lasting benefit to society, yet in whose lives there have been episodes that point an equally salutary if less melancholy moral. So numerous are the instances of intense artistic activity coupled with indifference to certain generally accepted ethical sanctions, that it is not strange that many should incline to the belief that it is the natural tendency of the æsthetic passion to undermine the foundations of the sterner virtues.

Such a conclusion is grossly exaggerated and can be held only in company with a superficial view of the nature of art and its history. It cannot be denied, however, that there are peculiar temptations against which the art enthusiast and the artist also should be fortified. The artist and the art lover live in an ideal world, and their elevation above the prosaic routine of ordinary life seems often to lift them above the conventional virtues and obligations. Examples of ethical unconcern in union with superior artistic achievement occur most conspicuously in those periods of art, such as the Renaissance and the nineteenth century romantic epoch, when all the conditions stimulated an intense individualism. In periods such as that of the Gothic architecture and sculpture, where the artist works upon general ideas and hides himself in production of a common type, the artist's temper is serene because he feels no antagonism. The artists of the Renaissance and the romantic period, on the other hand, were in arms against an established order, and the latter especially, in defying traditional authority and asserting independence in emotion and its expression, were frequently led into revolt against social usages which seemed to them involved in the Philistinism against which they waged a sort of holy war. License in matters of conduct seemed to them a logical corollary from the freedom of thought which they rightly claimed. A somewhat similar error will beguile the eager connoisseur if he is not on his guard. Even when actual moral relaxation does not ensue, there may be a luxurious abandonment to a one-sided culture which entails impatience with humdrum responsibilities, and eventually an enervation of that motive force that is needed for the efficient performance of commonplace domestic and social duties. The art voluptuary is always in danger of falling into that state of which Gautier speaks when he says of Gérard de Nerval that "the progressive invasion of dreams had gradually rendered it impossible for him to live in an environment where realities move."

The life of an artist offers a compensation for his frequent loss of hold upon external fact; he puts his emotion into form, he creates another fact, often so pure and lovely that his own detachment becomes a virtue because it is a necessary condition of a productiveness so beneficial. The dilettante, on the other hand, receives and enjoys at the cost of another's toil, while himself producing nothing. He often sinks into a state in which effort, for the time being at least, would be a burden, and the very work that was brought into existence with labor and pain may become to him a cause of languor and apathy.

Does this homily, it may be asked, at all concern

the music lover? Is there any risk in the musical infatuation equal to that which often lies in the other æsthetic cravings? On one side of the indictment a defense can be entered. The fact that "music arouses emotion without furnishing any hint of an end to which the emotion shall be directed," instead of constituting an especial snare, it seems to me comes near being a saving grace. Poetry and painting present to the imagination and the sight not only emotions, but objects and ends. This music cannot do. I am aware that many hold the belief that music can be moral or immoral, religious or irreligious *per se*. This is an error that is closely related to the notion that music alone can represent or describe actual concrete objects and definite sentiments. The demoralizing influence which some ascribe to the music of certain operas is not in the music, but (if it exists at all) in the texts and situations. A degrading idea may be associaated with a musical strain, but the probability is that this idea will fade away when the music is recalled. Music has a wonderful cleansing property. Professor George Santayana's statement that "art registers passions without stimulating them," and that "in stopping to depict them it steals away their life," — while somewhat in excess of the truth in respect to literature and the representative arts, is very near the truth in respect to music. It is doubtful if music has the power of registering passion; it can hardly even suggest it unless one is predetermined to find it there. Certain it is that music often throws over an unworthy theme a veil of such magical illusion that ugliness is turned into beauty, vice into purity. It is her glory that when permitted to act in freedom her communications are always innocent. We may call music good or bad, but we mean that it is well or ill composed. We may call it strong or weak, noble or trivial, refined or coarse, but we use these terms in a musical sense, not attaching to them any notion of approbation or disapprobation on ethical grounds. Sensuous desire and gross intrigue disappear from Beaumarchais's "Marriage of Figaro" when Mozart exorcizes the evil spirit by the touch of his happy, guileless music. Many people find it hard to accept these statements; the music has become so blended in their minds with the idea or picture that has been arbitrarily attached to it that they impute the effect of one to the other. Moreover, those who philosophize are often more prone to imagine experiences of others than to make an exact study of their own.

All this seems to me so plain that when I find even learned musical critics imputing ethical or unethical qualities to abstract music without words, scene, or even title, I confess myself sorely bewildered. A well known writer of our day finds Chopin's music "saturated with the color and mood of sex." Schumann's D minor symphony is "that obvious autobiography of triumphant love." Notice the word "obvious." Brahms, Liszt, Raff, Tchaikovsky "were thrall beyond any other allegiance to the persuasions of sexual emotion; music makers haunted and enchained by the glamour of the erotic." The writer is not offering this as a mere subjective impression — the erotic music of these men, he asserts, "makes no concealment, as it admits no doubt of its origin." Is there not here an odd jumble of psychologic and æsthetic confusions? The music of Brahms (Brahms the austere, Brahms the academic, so often pedantic, so often, we must confess it, dull) making no concealment and admitting no doubt of its origin in sexual emotion! Perhaps, also, certain music is pea-green, while other music smells of heliotrope or garlic, — such asseverations have been solemnly made. There is harm in such lucubrations as I have quoted because they mislead many confiding music lovers, persuading them, it may be, that poison lurks in a thing that is really pure, and this is almost as reprehensible a disservice as to persuade one that a harmful thing is innocent. A unique property of music is in that plasticity which enables it to take whatever stamp the fancy may choose to impress upon it. It suffers the hearer to conjure up whatever imagery his temperament or his theory may suggest; but when he is enthralled by visions that seem to him to assume reality within this tone world of magic, let him consider that he is entangled, like Merlin, in spells of his own weaving.

In this realm of the impalpable, toward which music so smilingly beckons, there may be pitfalls concealed among the flowers. But we shall not escape them by wholly misconceiving their nature.

When we speak of an emotion without an object, objectionable because there is no outlet afforded for instant action, we are in danger of falling into the trap that lies in an uncertain meaning given to the word emotion. To feel pity at the sight of real suffering, and then let it evaporate in tearful regret taking no trouble to relieve,—such abortive emotion is more likely to weaken than fortify the character. But when we use the word emotion to signify the mental stirring before a work of art, it carries very different connotations. The feelings aroused by a drama are not the feelings that would be aroused by corresponding incidents in real life. The illusionized spectator in the story, who leaped upon the stage to assault the successful villain, quite misunderstood the province of art. The murder of Desdemona has not the horror of reality. The loves of Antony and Cleopatra do not tempt us to emulation of their unholy excess; and it is not the warning of the tragic consequence that defeats the evil suggestion, but the intellectualizing, idealizing power of poetry. It is hardly correct to say that the emotion felt in music and other noble art has no end to which it may be directed. It is itself an end in the same sense that a religious emotion is itself an end. No one is reasonably required to turn every high mood into an instantaneous impulse to action. If this mood, whether it comes from music or any other pure source, makes one to any extent or in any particular a better man, then a worthy end is served. The deeds will follow when the proper occasion comes for them. And so music, while it may not arouse a zeal for speedy effort, may yet have other offices not less worthy. Through its power to soothe and refresh, to symbolize what is pure and holy, to promote the social consciousness by effecting a sense of fellowship with others in a refined experience, to brace the mind for coming duties by the tonic of joy, to lighten care and soften the hardness of adversity — through these blessed ministries has music earned the praises which the wise ones of the earth have always lavished upon her as an inspiring ally in moral culture and humanitarian progress. When a man feels himself thus exalted by music, when the glow of tenderness pervades his being as he goes home from a concert hall, he should not be ready to banish the impression. Even so kindly an act as speaking genially to his aunt would be wrong for him were it to bring him down abruptly from the soul's height which, as Wordsworth reminds us, is so difficult to keep.

In view of the conditions that prevail in this country and the mental habits of our people, it does not appear that either music or any other form of art is destined soon to become an influence that makes for social anæmia. But we may reach that point at last. If one uses art in such a way that it becomes a de-intellectualizing agency, to the demoralizing stage is only a step. The national reproach lies in the fact that, while we are beginning to encourage art, we use it as a detail in our pursuit of ostentation and pleasure, not for the incorporation of noble ideals or as an element in the dissemination of such ideals among the various ranks of society. We have not learned to take art seriously; we have no distinct knowledge of the purpose that the arts, when made a part of religion and patriotic aspiration, have fulfilled in history; we have no resolute ambition to bring them into the deeper currents of our life. A superficial dilettantism is still characteristic of many who take notice of art, while the attitude of the great majority is that of stupid disrespect. It may be that this indifference is slowly giving way, but if so the danger is that those who leave the crowd of the obtuse and join the circle of the amateurs will do so without bringing with them any very stern determination to use art as a means of adding to the true riches of the soul. The gain is not great if there is merely a multiplication of the horde that sees only the sensuous side of art, skimming its surface for a taste of momentary delectation, finding nothing that strengthens the understanding or reënforces the agencies that make for enlightenment and virtue.

So far as music is concerned (and the rules of health are the same in all the arts) the individual's safeguard against the enfeeblement which may result from over-indulgence in the sweets of this most intoxicating of æsthetic enjoyments is, it seems to me, twofold. In the first place we may say, paraphrasing a well known maxim respecting the evils of democracy, that the cure for the possible ills of music is more music. By this I mean more music of the highest order, together with a preparation of mind that enables one to discriminate between the qualities that fade and the qualities that endure, and an artistic conscience that refuses to find satisfaction in work that is not sincerely felt and skilfully wrought. Anything less than this is injustice to one's self, injustice to the art, and injustice to the musician who asks that he shall not be exposed to the temptation of degrading his work in order that he may live.

In the second place, the conscientious amateur will escape the danger that lies in wait for those who are too much at ease in the musical Zion, if he will add his own momentum to those blessed efforts, that are springing up all over this country, to bring the sweet companionship of music to those who live far from the centres of culture, to those who are forming their taste in colleges and schools, and to those who toil with their hands for daily bread. In this age of humanitarian endeavor, he is indeed an alert observer who can count the movements for the welfare of men which make their appearance every day; it would not be strange if he overlooked the efforts which are organized in many of our cities for the musical benefit of the masses. This is not the place to enumerate them or to describe the happy results that flow from them. It is enough to say that the common belief that the people prefer bad music to good is everywhere refuted. The tribute that has been paid by a prominent critic to the service of the People's Symphony concerts in New York would be applicable to other similar institutions. In speaking of the large and enthusiastic audiences he says: "These people are learning what music is; what the composers have created and set before them for the information of their intellect and the warning of their imagination. They are true and humble and devoted music lovers, and in their homes the tone art will be a part of the daily thought of their children and come into its own."

In spite of the influences that are now in action for the dissemination of good music among all the social groups, the taste of the vast majority is still debased, and the amount of vulgar, trashy music heard at the thousands of cheap pleasure resorts is appalling. Yet there is comfort in the belief that the masses seize eagerly upon music of the "cheap and nasty" variety because they have not been able to hear any other. Good music, at least decent music, prevails when it is given a chance, and although Gresham's law may be true in the world of finance it has no counterpart in the world of tone. No one ever devoted himself with unselfish zeal to the improvement of the public taste who did not find encouragement, and, if he persevered, a reward beyond his hopes. Philanthropists have only just begun to see what the elevation of the people's amusements would do for public contentment and public morals. Here is a field in which all can try experiments. One result at least is sure,— any one will find that his artistic pleasures will contribute to his moral growth if he seeks cordially to share them with his neighbor. If any harm ever comes from the indulgence of a love for art it will be because that love is egotistic, because it loses sight of the fact that the enjoyment of one, however refined and pure it may appear to be, is a delusion unless it is of such a kind that it can unite with the interest of all.

At the end of this long argument framed for the justification of the study of music to the reason, and in deprecation of certain deductions which something in music's nature seems so prone to encourage, the feeling comes over me that I have played an ungrateful, half-treacherous part in seeming to imply that any apology should ever be needed for whole souled devotion to this queenliest and most beneficent of the arts. When her pure accents fall upon our ears, transmitted to us by those prophets and high priests of Beauty whom we call composers, when our whole being trembles with a joy which we know contains no admixture of evil because it is not of the world in which our feet stumble and our hands are soiled,— in these rapt moments we may easily be moved to think that our hard won scientific lore, our calm critical appraisals, are after all impertinent, for what can music ask of us, what can anything fair and holy ask of us, except unsuspicious acceptance and glad surrender? If we are told, while still under the sway of some sublime harmony, that music is of inferior worth because it is detached from life, we are tempted to ask our monitor, with something like indignation, what he means by life; if there is no life except what we can see and touch; and whence, if not from life — life that is very full, very rich, and near to the centre of Being — can a communication of such ineffable beauty proceed?

There is something inferior and partial in a phase of life that has nothing in it to which music can suggest a counterpart, for music, more than any other form of human expression, tells us of a sphere into which we can rise where contradictions are removed and discords resolved. Perhaps the mystics to whom I have referred, such as Thoreau and Hearn, who are lifted by music "above the mire and dust of the universe," hearing "reminders of our destiny," who are haunted in music by "the pains and joys of lives innumerable," — perhaps they have seen more deeply than the critics and theorists and are the true soothsayers. It is the unique praise of music that the humble and suffering ones, in every age and in every land, have sought in the folk song for abiding consolation; that religion has found her offices of worship grow cold when deprived of music's presence; that patriotism has found in melody its most potent stimulus to heroic deed; that every phase of domestic life, from the cradle to the grave, has always and everywhere been sweetened and sanctified by this blessed ministry. It has ever been the purpose of music to increase the joy of the world. In the last analysis this is the supreme aim of all art and its chiefest glory; and what words can there be that are eloquent enough to give sufficient honor to whatever helps to convince men that they are born for happiness? And thus every man who brings beauty nearer to his fellows and makes them love it more is a missionary of a sacred cause, a herald of peace and good will.

There are agencies that lift men into moods that are blithe and hopeful, in which strength is renewed and faith rekindled, and one of them is music. In spite of exceptions so rare that they emphasize the rule, it is a fact of deep significance that music, the universal art, to which men have confided the most cherished experiences of their souls, is an art that tells of gladness. The student of the world's literature is constantly touching a vein of disillusion and despair, and his contact with many of its rarest minds often leaves him depressed. But at the sound of music cares and distresses are overborne, and the soul is set adrift on a tide that flows toward radiant horizons. Not that music has no sympathy with sorrow, but when she enters into places of mourning she does so not to make more poignant the agony of grief, but rather to console. And this triumph of the soul of which music testifies is no mere distraction, bringing false comfort by concealing the truth. It imparts strength because its majestic movement tells of tireless power; it opens vistas of hope because its golden tones bear no trace of the discordant sounds of earthly struggle and lamenting.

Let us not fear, then, lest we bestow too much thought upon music, or lest we be overzealous in furthering its interests in the community. We have only to watch that we love it wisely, study it broadly and seriously, train our perceptions to catch the whole of its meaning and not a fragment, strive to discover the relation of music to life, and not vainly imagine that he honors music, or does good service to himself, who takes the flattering unction to his soul that his taste separates him from those who lack what he is pleased to call culture. Art, when rightly understood, promotes fraternity and not exclusiveness. The revival of art and its adoption into the system of popular education is a sign of health in our age, and to it every loyal citizen should give heed and lend his aid in bringing its benefits close to the public need. His preparation for this service, when the art of music is involved, will be first of all in his education as a true music lover. He will seek association with the great tone masters, he will confidingly yield his spirit to the healthful currents that flow from their strong spirits. He will so nourish his musical appreciations that his consciousness of the vital things in the art will flourish with his general mental growth, with his advancement in taste, with his increasing reverence for all things that are excellent and fair. Convinced that strength and enlargement come from music when its social and individual quickening power is rightly applied, he will find the warrant of his discipleship in the zeal to assist every unselfish effort to open highways for this emissary of good in its gladsome errand among men.

APPENDIX

THE following is an incomplete list of non-technical books that will prove valuable to the amateur music lover. Histories, biographies, dictionaries, and text books are not included. Should the reader wish to extend his researches further, he will find in the author's *The Study of the History of Music* a very ample list of works touching all sides of musical knowledge.

Ambros (A. W.). *The Boundaries of Music and Poetry.* Tr. by Cornell. New York: Schirmer, 1893.

Baughan (E. A.). *Music and Musicians.* London: Lane, 1906.

Coerne (L. A.). *The Evolution of Modern Orchestration.* New York: Macmillan, 1908.

Combarieu (Jules). *Music, Its Laws and Evolution.* International Scientific Series. New York: Appleton, 1910.

Ffrangcon-Davies (David). *The Singing of the Future.* London: Lane, 1906.

Finck (H. T.). *Chopin and Other Musical Essays.* New York: Scribner, 1894.

——. *Songs and Song Writers.* New York: Scribner, 1900.

——. *Success in Music and How It Is Won.* New York: Scribner, 1909.

Gilman (Lawrence). *Phases of Modern Music.* New York: Harper, 1904.

Gilman (Lawrence). *Stories of Symphonic Music: A Guide to the Meaning of Important Symphonies, Overtures, and Tone Poems from Beethoven to the Present Day.* New York: Harper, 1904.

Glyn (Margaret H). *The Rhythmic Conception of Music.* New York: Longmans, Green & Co., 1907.

Grove (George). *Beethoven and His Nine Symphonies.* London: Novello, 1896.

Gurney (Edmund). *The Power of Sound.* London: Smith, Elder & Co., 1880.

Hadow (W. H.). *Studies in Modern Music.* 2 vols. New York: Macmillan, 1892–3.

Hale (Philip), editor and author. *Program Books of the Boston Symphony Orchestra.* Published annually by C. A. Ellis.

Henderson (W. J.). *Modern Musical Drift.* New York: Longmans, 1904.

——. *Preludes and Studies.* New York: Longmans, 1891

——. *The Art of the Singer.* New York: Scribner, 1906.

——. *The Orchestra and Orchestral Music.* New York: Scribner, 1899.

——. *What is Good Music?* New York: Scribner, 1898.

Kobbè (Gustav). *How to Appreciate Music.* New York: Moffat, Yard & Co., 1910.

Krehbiel (H. E.). *How to Listen to Music.* New York: Scribner, 1897.

Lavignac (Albert). *Music and Musicians.* Tr. by Marchant. New York: Holt, 1905.

Mason (D. G.). *A Guide to Music.* New York: Baker & Taylor Co., 1910.

——. *The Orchestral Instruments and What They Do.* New York: Baker & Taylor Co., 1910.

Mason (D. G.) and Surette (T. W.). *The Appreciation of Music.* New York: Baker & Taylor Co., 1910.

(An explanation of the chief musical forms, with special reference to the works of Bach and Beethoven.)

APPENDIX

Mees (Arthur). *Choirs and Choral Music.* New York: Scribner, 1901.

Newman (Ernest). *Musical Studies.* London: Lane, 1905.

Niecks (Frederick). *Programme Music in the Last Four Centuries.* London: Novello, 1907.

Parry (C. H. H.). *The Evolution of the Art of Music.* New York: Appleton, 1896.

Pole (William). *The Philosophy of Music.* London: Trübner, 1879.

(An explanation of the principles of musical science.)

Riemann (Hugo). *Catechism of Musical Æsthetics.* Tr. by Berewunge. London: Augener, no date.

——. *Dictionary of Music.* Tr. by Shedlock. London: Augener.

Symons (Arthur). *Studies in Seven Arts.* New York: Dutton, 1906.

Upton (G. P.). *The Standard Concert Guide: A Handbook of the Standard Symphonies, Oratorios, Cantatas, and Symphonic Poems for the Concert Goer.* Chicago: McClurg, 1908.

——. *The Standard Operas.* Chicago: McClurg, 1908.

Wagner (Richard). *On Conducting.* Tr. by Dannreuther. London: Reeves, 1887.

Wallaschek (Richard). *Primitive Music.* London: Longmans, 1893.